SETTING SAIL
TEN THOUSAND YEARS OF SEAFARING ADVENTURE

Cuyvers, Luc
Setting Sail: Ten Thousand Years of Seafaring Adventure

Copyright © 2004 by Luc Cuyvers
Published by Tide-mark Press, Ltd.
Windsor, Connecticut

All Rights Reserved under International and Pan American Copyright Conventions

First North American Edition

Library of Congress Cataloging-in-Publication Data
Cuyvers, Luc
Setting Sail
p. 174
Includes Index

ISBN: 1-55949-879-X

Library of Congress Control Number
2003113661

Printed in Korea

LUC CUYVERS

SETTING SAIL

TEN THOUSAND YEARS OF SEAFARING ADVENTURE

CONTENTS

INTRODUCTION

History bears no record of where or when the first boat was built. It is somewhat irrelevant anyway. After all, boats weren't "invented" by any one person at any specific time. Instead, different people in different places gradually developed them, using available materials. In some areas they used trees; in others they searched for reeds or other materials that provided sufficient buoyancy.

Once they discovered they could sit on a floating log or on reeds strung together, people in different regions figured out that they could use their hands or a stick to go somewhere. They did not necessarily do so at the same time. Some were quick to grasp the possibilities; others took a little longer. But there is little doubt that, before they learned to write or do any of the other things we generally associate with "civilization," people had ventured out on the water. We don't know what enticed early people to do so, although it is tempting to speculate. Perhaps it was to seek food or to flee invaders. Or perhaps simply to wander and explore what lay beyond the horizon. For people seeking mobility, rivers offered convenient pathways through seemingly impenetrable areas.

People also used floating objects to move at sea long before recorded history. As long as half a million years ago, they went from Africa into Europe across the Mediterranean Sea. Even the shortest route, across the Strait of Gibraltar, stretched six miles—a distance probably crossed with log floats. Much greater distances were covered by the people who occupied Australia from Southeast Asia at least forty thousand years ago. During the Ice Ages, when sea levels were much lower than they are today, stretches of water of up to fifty miles separated the islands that became stepping-stones to the vast Australian landmass.

With the onset of organized life some ten thousand years ago, boats and rafts began taking on an additional role. Rather than being merely a means of getting from one place to another, boats could also carry people's goods and supplies. Not only that, they did so far more efficiently than anything else and did not require roads, of which there were very few anyway. It is not surprising then that the first great centers of civilization developed along rivers and coastlines. And it is no wonder that the means to move safely on water became one of their inhabitants' principal quests.

This book is about this ten-thousand-year-old quest, though not from a conventional perspective. Having been written mostly by Western experts, much of maritime history tends to focus on the seafaring feats of Western people, as if they were the only ones that mattered. That is nonsense. Western mariners would eventually dominate much of the sea, but there were other great seafaring traditions whose exploits were no less impressive, and often achieved much earlier. Being less well documented, non-Western achievements are often ignored, though that leads to a rather one-sided view of the story of people and the sea.

To redress that situation, this book also outlines the maritime history of some important non-Western cultures. But it does so out of more than merely a desire to present a complete picture. The story of seafaring simply cannot be viewed as an isolated development. Though people's first steps at sea occurred in separate places, it didn't take long before ideas began to be exchanged, first among neighboring islands, then among nearby regions, and before long even between continents.

And thus, along with goods, people, and cargoes came new ideas. Always eager to reduce risks at sea, seafarers observed one another. If one came up with a good idea, there was a good chance others would adopt it. Very good ideas eventually made their way throughout the world. There are some classic examples of this transfer of technology, such as the compass making its way from Song Dynasty China to Europe via Arab middlemen. The compass obviously was a good idea. The moment it became available, no mariner wanted to leave port without it.

Rigging designs too made their way around the world. Here the Arabs played a role as well, introducing the triangular lateen sail first to Mediterranean seafarers, from whence it made its way further north. It proved a monumental development. Without some form of fore-and-aft rigging, which allowed for better progress into the wind, European mariners would have been hard pressed to venture on their worldwide explorations.

Other ideas took a remarkably long time to take hold. The stern rudder, for instance, took more than one thousand years to make its way from China to the West, even though it was a far more efficient steering device than the steering oar European sailors used until the late Middle Ages. The Chinese tradition of building ships with watertight compartments took even longer to make its way west. It was described by European travelers, among them Marco Polo, who thought it an outstanding idea. And yet, watertight bulkheads were not included in Western vessels for another couple of centuries. Innumerable ships and lives would have been saved if the practice had been adopted earlier.

It is not entirely clear why some ideas were adopted readily while others were ignored. Superstition and a stubborn sense of tradition may have had something to do with it. In some respects sailors are notoriously conservative, and not necessarily eager to adopt something they have not thought of themselves. Even so, there is no question that the story of ships and seafaring is one of technological intercourse. Looking at it from a regional perspective yields no more than a partial picture at best.

Examining seafaring from a variety of cultural angles reveals more than intriguing exchange patterns. It also demonstrates a variety of approaches to the same challenge. The people of Southeast Asia and the Pacific, for instance, came up with a unique ship design. Like people elsewhere, they probably started out with a dugout tree trunk, to which they later added a sail. But sails tend to make dugouts notoriously unstable. To counter that, they added outrigger floats, not unlike the training wheels on a child's bicycle. Later that design developed into a single outrigger or a double-hulled canoe; a remarkably swift vessel, as any recreational sailor can attest.

People in Europe, the Middle East, and China dealt with the problem in a different way. Rather than adding outriggers, they built up their canoes' freeboards and then added a good deal of weight at the bottom to provide stability. The result was the displacement hull common to Western ships, as well as to dhows and to junks. Since people there were interested in transporting cargoes, it is tempting to speculate that they developed their ships in response to the need for space. But there may be more to it than that. People in the Near East and Far East learned the art of ships and shipping on the relative calm of rivers. In the Pacific, on the other hand, people had to deal with the motion of the sea. That probably forced them to come up with a more radical solution, and thus a very different type of vessel.

Each of the cultures examined in this book had its own adjustments to particular challenges. The Austronesians and Polynesians not only came up with swift catamarans, they also developed unique navigational techniques. To the sailors of the Middle East and Indian Ocean probably goes the honor of conceiving of the lateen sail, though similar designs may have been developed independently in Southeast Asia. China came up with a wealth of innovations, many of them reportedly observed from nature. In fact, just about anything the Chinese incorporated into their vessels, much of it later admired in the West, can be found along a Chinese pond. A leaf skirting along the surface, according to tradition, provided the inspiration for sail. Bamboo not only provided a splendid floating material, its compartments also gave rise to the idea of watertight bulkheads. A carp flipping its tail led to the development of a steering device placed at the stern of a ship, rather than somewhere along its quarter.

These are just a few examples of regional ingenuity. Some eventually became part of nautical technology worldwide; most never did, but that doesn't make them less interesting. These advances reveal as much about the people who thought of them as they do about their ships. Unless we look at the story of seafaring in a multi-cultural context, we are likely to overlook these developments.

The lack of published information on other seafaring cultures is not just the result of the West's nautical arrogance. As we shall see in the chapters ahead, there is little to justify ignoring what others achieved at sea. But no matter how open-minded, anyone interested in global maritime history is seriously hindered by a serious shortage of sources. The Polynesians, for instance, didn't leave us a single text, other than what was written down after Europeans first recorded their stories. Aside from a few faded rock carvings, there are no images of their craft. Not a single one of their great voyaging canoes has survived either, leaving many of their seafaring exploits in a semi-permanent state of speculation.

The sailors of the Middle East and Indian Ocean were remarkably tight-lipped as well. The Arabs, who controlled the sea trade between East and West for more than five hundred years, didn't leave a single decent picture of one of their great trading dhows, for instance. As far as their writings are concerned, there are a few accounts, though most of them have a heavy dose of mythology thrown in for good measure. Compared to the extent of their trading, the visual and written records of their activities are minuscule. Arab sailors, it seemed, simply were not interested in leaving documents about their everyday maritime doings.

The situation is somewhat better in China, though there the mercurial nature of the imperial bureaucracy often led to the destruction of invaluable records. As a result, there is relatively little factual information on China's early maritime history and, in comparison to its significance, hardly anything on its great age of nautical exploration. Although more materials may surface in the future, until they are translated and made accessible, the story of China and the sea will remain incomplete.

The maritime history of the West, in contrast, is a veritable treasure trove, filled as it is with records, stories, eyewitness accounts, paintings, mosaics, reliefs, and just about anything else from the days of ancient Greece onward. One could argue that this wealth of information results from history being written by the victors, but that isn't true. Much of this was documented when Western maritime technology remained far behind that of other cultures—when there was not even a hint of a dominant maritime position, in other words. It thus appears that Western people were more interested than others in maintaining some sort of record of their dealings with the sea. That is reason for pride because it correctly recognizes that the sea taught us more than how to get from one place to another. But it is no reason to be smug and ignore what others achieved at sea.

It is hoped this book provides a small step in the right direction.

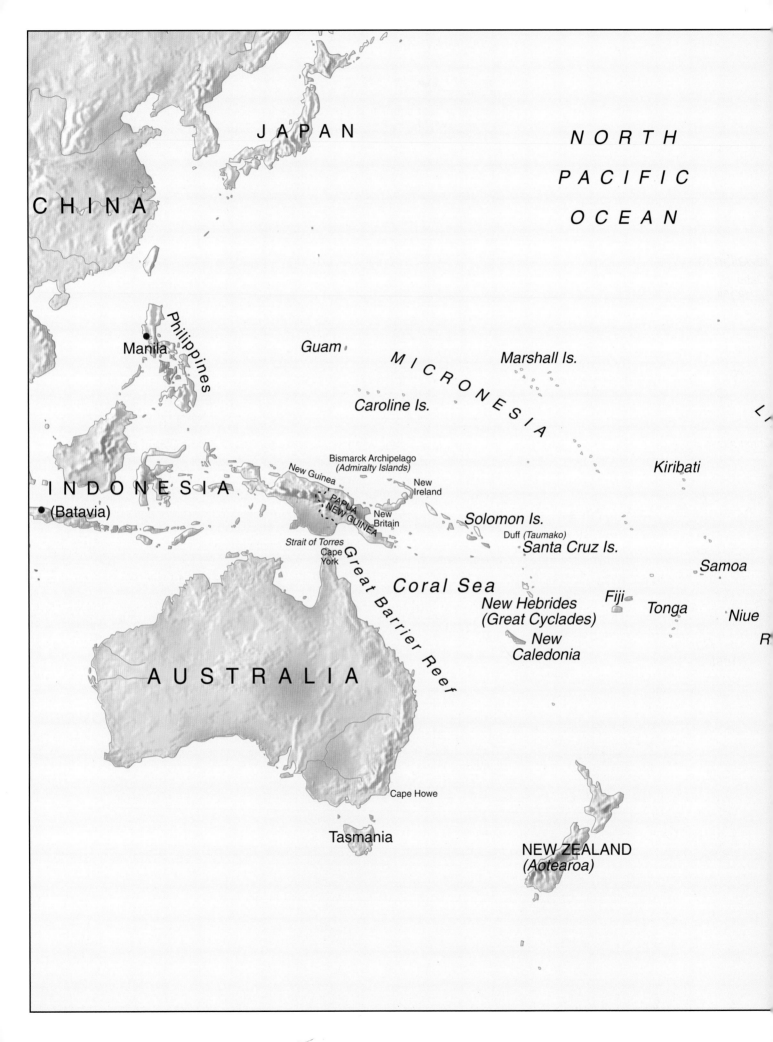

CHINA

JAPAN

NORTH

PACIFIC

OCEAN

Manila

Philippines

Guam

Marshall Is.

M I C R O N E S I A

Caroline Is.

Kiribati

INDONESIA

(Batavia)

New Guinea

Bismarck Archipelago
(Admiralty Islands)

New
Ireland

PAPUA
NEW GUINEA

New
Britain

Solomon Is.

Duff *(Taumako)*

Santa Cruz Is.

Strait of Torres

Cape
York

Great Barrier Reef

Coral Sea

New Hebrides
(Great Cyclades)

Fiji

Tonga

Samoa

Niue

New
Caledonia

AUSTRALIA

Cape Howe

Tasmania

NEW ZEALAND
(Aotearoa)

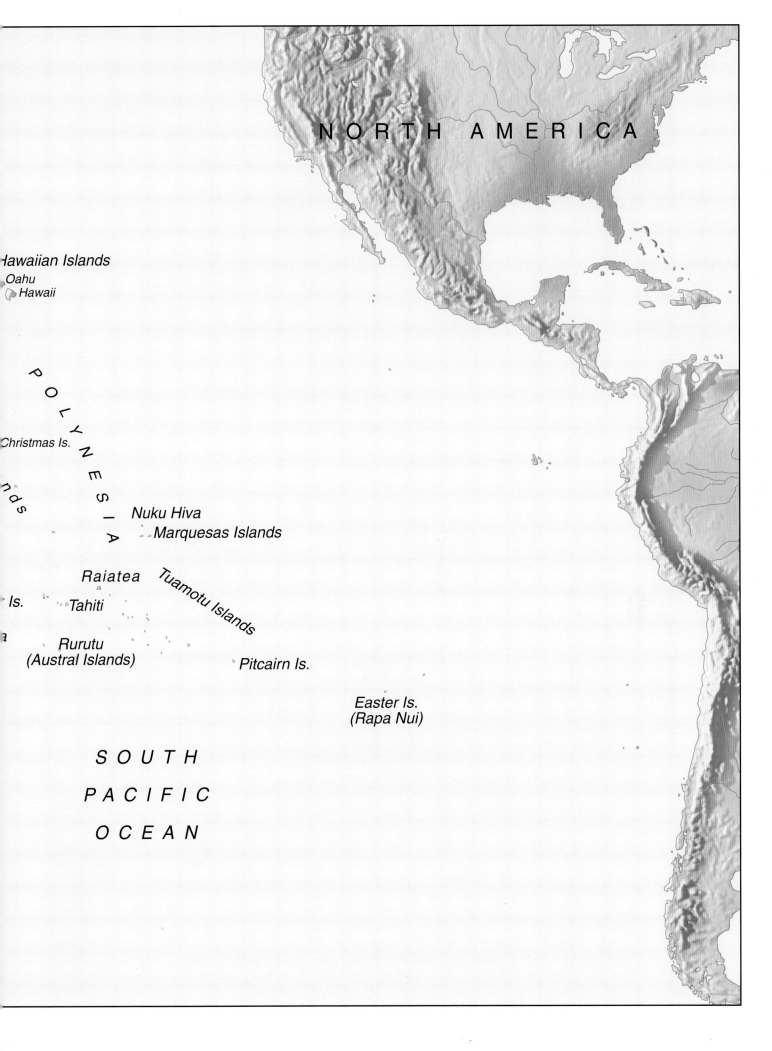

THE GREAT VOYAGERS

'In these proes or pahees as they call them, these people sail in those seas from island to island for several hundred leagues, the Sun serving them for a compass by day and the Moon and Stars by night. When this comes to be proved we shall no longer be at a loss to know how the islands in those seas came to be peopled, for if the inhabitants of these islands have been at islands laying 2 or 300 Leagues to the West, it cannot be doubted that the inhabitants of those islands may have been at others as far westward of them, and so we may trace them from island to island quite to the East Indies.'

These are the words of James Cook, one of the world's greatest explorers, as recorded in the journal of his first voyage to the Pacific (1768-1771). Impressed with the geographic range of a people he had encountered from Tahiti to New Zealand, Cook speculated about their origins, suggesting they migrated across the Pacific from Southeast Asia. Given the prevailing European attitude that these "savages" could hardly find their way around their own islands, not to mention the uncharted ocean, his was a bold thesis but it proved on the mark. "These people," or Polynesians as they would later become known, were indeed capable of traveling long distances at sea. They did use the sky as a means to orient themselves in open seas, and their forebears had come from the East Indies, against prevailing winds and currents. It took someone like Cook, himself a superb sailor and navigator, to appreciate this achievement.

Key to the realization that the people of Tahiti and New Zealand belonged to a single cultural entity was the observation that, aside from physical features, they shared the same language. When Cook arrived in New Zealand, for instance, he found that the local Maoris immediately understood his Tahitian guide. Discovering that they also shared customs and religious beliefs, he correctly concluded that they "had one origin or source." But Cook had seen only part of the picture.

On his second voyage to the Pacific (1772-1775), Cook sailed further south than anyone had before in search of the southern continent that many scientists expected to be there. Once that proved unsuccessful, he headed north again, to look

for "imperfectly explored" islands, that is, places that had been visited by Europeans before but had never been adequately charted. Key among them was isolated Easter Island, which had been "discovered" by Dutch navigator Jacob Roggeveen on Easter Sunday in 1722. No European had visited it in the fifty years since.

By starting out far to the east and then running along Roggeveen's reported latitude, Cook was able to reach Easter Island. But he and his men were utterly unprepared for what came next. The people who came out to greet them spoke a language similar to that of the Tahitians and Maoris, and shared similar customs. This puzzled Cook because he could not see any boat or canoe longer than ten feet, but there was no question in his mind about the Easter Islanders' origins. "It is extraordinary that the same Nation should have spread themselves over all the islands in this vast ocean from New Zealand to this Island, which is almost a fourth of the circumference of the globe," he later wrote in his journal.

The final and most astounding piece of the Polynesian puzzle fell into place on Cook's third voyage to the Pacific (1776-1779). Heading north from Tahiti, Cook did not anticipate running into any more Polynesians. After all, the Tahitians did not seem to know of major islands further north, and Cook was not sure whether more existed. But six weeks and more than two thousand miles from Tahiti, his men sighted high, mountainous islands. When they drew near, a number of people paddled out in canoes to greet them. To Cook's utter amazement, they spoke the same language too.

Dawn breaks on an island in Southeast Asia. From here the ancestors of the Polynesians departed into the vast expanse of the Pacific.

James Cook was the first person to acknowledge the full extent of the Polynesian diaspora and one of the first to pay tribute to the Polynesians' nautical achievements. Dispersed from New Zealand in the south to Easter Island in the east and Hawaii in the north, these people had sailed across thousands of miles of open ocean, without charts, instruments, or anything else Western sailors would have considered essential. More importantly, they had done so at a time when mariners elsewhere were barely venturing out of sight of land. "How shall we account for this Nation spreading itself so far over this vast ocean?" Cook later wondered.

Unfortunately he never had a chance to come up with a detailed answer. A few months later Cook was dead, killed on the shore of the big island of Hawaii in a skirmish over a stolen boat. The West lost one of its greatest explorers, the Polynesians in all likelihood one of their greatest advocates.

THE FIRST NAVIGATORS

"How shall we account for this Nation spreading itself so far over this vast ocean?" The question has kept historians, archaeologists, and anthropologists occupied since Cook first phrased it, and it has by no means been totally resolved.

Of course, research has revealed a great deal, especially in the last twenty or thirty years. Both traditional and experimental archaeology have enabled historians to partially answer when and how the Polynesians fanned out across the Pacific. There also is widespread agreement over the general pattern of the Polynesian diaspora—a pattern that consists of several eastward thrusts, first from Fiji to Tonga and Samoa, from there to the Marquesas, and thence far beyond to Easter Island. Also from the Marquesas, a separate group of travelers went north to Hawaii, and west to Tahiti and the rest of the Society Islands. And from there travelers completed the final thrust south to New Zealand around A.D. 800.

The absence of written and visual records documenting this migration leaves room for speculation, but there now is general agreement that the Polynesians left their various bases in the western Pacific well before the Christian era to set out into an expanse of ocean twice the size of the continental United States. Considering that people elsewhere—even in the highly advanced cultures of China, the Indus Valley, Egypt, and the Mediterranean—seldom sailed out of sight of land, it was an outstanding achievement. There is no question that *these people* were the world's first great blue-water sailors, and that they will forever rank among its greatest voyagers.

Of course, the further one reaches back in time, the hazier the picture. Though it is possible to trace the origins of the Polynesian expansion to the islands of the western Pacific, how did the people who lived there reach these islands in the first place? And where did they come from?

The story involves two migrations. The first took place some forty thousand or even fifty thousand years ago, and involved groups of people from Southeast Asia migrating to New Guinea and Australia. Because of the Ice Age, sea levels were much lower than they are today, creating land bridges that linked New Guinea and Australia into a large landmass. Even so, these early migrants had to cross sea channels between some of the Indonesian islands, and continue from there to New Guinea. We have no idea how they did that, other than by assuming they used primitive rafts of bamboo or logs. To do so, and then to survive successfully on the other side, undoubtedly took more planning and organization than we usually associate with Neolithic people.

This first wave of migrants consisted of Australoid people, now known as Melanesians, with dark skin, wooly hair, and a wiry build. Most settled in Australia and New Guinea, but much later some moved east into the Pacific, first to islands like New Britain and New Ireland northeast of New Guinea, then to the Solomon Islands, and finally to more distant places like the New Hebrides. These moves would have required advanced nautical capabilities, but the Melanesians were not a voyaging people. Instead they tended to settle wherever they arrived, first as hunter-gatherers in Australia and New Guinea, and later by developing primitive agricultural techniques, without which settlement on smaller islands would not have been possible.

About five thousand years ago, a second wave of migrants began to move east from Southeast Asia. Lighter skinned and with Asian features, these people looked different from the Melanesians. Known as Austronesians, they would become the ancestors of the Polynesians.

Though little is known about their earliest migration, it is believed that the Austronesians arrived in Southeast Asia from southern China, and then continued to move east. But how they did so is unknown. Considerable stretches of open water had to be crossed, suggesting a need for more than a drifting raft. In fact, there was no longer a way of doing so without some form of long-distance propulsion, suggesting that sail had been developed or introduced in Southeast Asia around this time.

The Feni islands in the Bismarck archipelago, north of Papua New-Guinea. Three thousand years ago a thriving Lapita community was established here. Its remnants are now being examined by Glenn Summerhayes of the Australian National University (right).

Why the Austronesians left is also unknown, though there is a possibility that the end of the last Ice Age caused population pressures by inundating low-lying areas. Elsewhere, too, rising sea levels triggered population moves, many of them accompanied by improvements in maritime technology. Unfortunately, while some evidence of these improvements was preserved in Europe and the Near East, none survived in the tropical Pacific. As a result, we know nothing about the rafts or canoes the Austronesians used on their first oceanic passages.

From their homes in Indonesia and possibly the Philippines, the Austronesians began their eastward thrust into the Pacific along the north coast of New Guinea, possibly following the routes initiated by the first migrants thousands of years earlier. At first, they reached places already occupied by Melanesian inhabitants. If there was sufficient food and space, they apparently cohabited peacefully. But settled island areas often provided a different situation. With land, fresh water, and other resources at a premium, the Austronesians moved on, well beyond the range of their Melanesian predecessors, and reached uninhabited islands further east.

The Austronesians did not leave any records of their nautical exploits. Fortunately, once they reached the islands northeast of New Guinea, they left something tangible. It began to be unearthed early in the past century, when German archaeologists discovered distinctive potsherds in ancient settlements in the Bismarck archipelago in northeastern Papua New Guinea. A few years later, similar sherds were found near Lapita in New Caledonia, and by the early 1920s they were discovered in Tonga as well. It was clear that the pottery had been made by the same group of people, who became known as the Lapita. But far more exciting, scientists soon discovered that radiocarbon dating of the sherds provided insight into the timing of these people's migration.

Potsherds do not offer insight into maritime technology, but they tell us a great deal more than might be anticipated. By carefully studying the various motifs, for instance, archaeologists have been able to figure out migration routes into the western Pacific and, more importantly, which groups seem to have stayed in touch with one another. Though they were not necessarily trading, it appears that communication occurred among some settlements, involving an exchange network of sorts. This, too, sheds light on the maritime capabilities of the Lapita people because the ability to voyage back and forth would have required fairly reliable vessels and skilled seamanship.

The distances that had to be covered also imply that the Lapita possessed advanced maritime technologies. On several occasions they had to cross stretches of open sea of several hundred miles. Between Fiji and Tonga there are nearly four hundred miles, for instance, and more than that between Fiji and Samoa. The voyage between the New Hebrides and Fiji is even larger: well over five hundred miles without a single island in between to break the passage. Despite the distances involved, all these places show clear evidence of a Lapita presence, established there in the course of the second millennium B.C.

THE POLYNESIAN EXPANSION

Lapita travelers probably reached Tonga between 1000 and 900 B.C., and Samoa one hundred to two hundred years later. What happened next is a matter of debate. Initially the assumption was that they settled these islands and remained there without further moves for between five hundred and one thousand years. During this time an ancestral Polynesian culture would have developed from its Lapita roots. Then, some time before the Christian era, the theory continues, they resumed their eastward thrust, first to the islands of the central Pacific and much later to the corners of the so-called Polynesian triangle: Easter Island, Hawaii, and New Zealand.

A more recent theory rejects that assumption, stipulating that the Lapita move into the Pacific continued essentially without interruption from the Bismarck archipelago off Papua New Guinea to central Polynesia. If true, settlers would have arrived in the Cook and Marquesas islands much earlier than originally believed. The evidence to confirm this theory, its proponents argue, may lie buried under sediments or have been submerged as a result of island subsidence.

Finally, there are also theories that set the arrival in the central Pacific much later, confirming that the debate over the Polynesian expansion is far from settled. The uncertainty derives in part from a change in cooking methods, as the original Lapita inhabitants of the western Pacific gradually switched from pottery to earth ovens (umus). With the pottery went the clues that allowed archaeologists to track the movements of their ancestors with some measure of confidence. Figuring out subsequent moves relies instead on carbon dating of organic material and, in many cases, on little more than vegetation changes revealed in sediment cores. This sort of evidence is not so easily interpreted as a potsherd, explaining why discussions over the timing of the Polynesian dispersal will probably continue for some time to come.

In spite of these varying views on its timing, there is some consensus that the second move eastward was to the islands of central Polynesia. These include the Cook, Marquesas, Society, Tuamotu, and Austral Islands.

One would logically assume that the early Polynesians settled the islands nearest to their departure point first, yet no archaeological evidence to that effect has been found. Everything unearthed thus far on the Cook Islands or the western islands of French Polynesia dates from the second half of the first millennium, long after the first Polynesians are believed to have left their islands in the western Pacific.

For that reason some archaeologists suspect that, after setting out from their homelands on Tonga and Samoa, one of the first groups of voyagers went as far as Nuku Hiva in the Marquesas, some two thousand miles upwind from their departure point. Initially scientists theorized that this would have taken place more than two thousand years ago, but later it became clear that their assumptions were based on imprecise dating of artifacts found amid the earliest levels of human occupation on Nuku Hiva. The arrival date moved up a couple hundred years, to about A.D. 300, based on a new set of carbon dates and on comparisons between the recovered artifacts and similar objects in the western Pacific.

Marquesan legends contain references to this original migration, but Westerners paid little attention to them. In fact, the first Europeans to arrive in the

Dark skin and wooly hair shows this young Bismarck Islander (left) to be Melanesian, a descendant of the first people to arrive in this part of the Pacific. The Polynesians, in contrast, are lighter skinned and possess Asian features (above).

area thought the idea of Marquesans traveling long distances absurd. Pedro Fernández de Quirós, who chanced upon the islands in 1595, did not believe a word of the natives' tales of long voyages. Noticing that they possessed no large sailing canoes or navigational instruments, he called them a "people without the possibility of sailing to distant parts." In de Quirós's view, the islanders probably came from the mysterious southern continent he had been ordered to find.

By the nineteenth century people knew that, aside from Antarctica, there was no southern continent, but the assumption then was that the Marquesans had arrived from Tahiti, some seven hundred miles southwest of Nuku Hiva. Native claims to the contrary were disregarded. Europeans simply found it too difficult to accept the idea that the islanders had sailed hundreds of miles into contrary winds and currents early in the Christian era. And yet Marquesan oral tradition not only told of the first voyage, it also explained why the original settlers bypassed a number of atolls along the way. According to one legend, the voyagers were looking for a mountainous island, perhaps Tahiti or another of the Society Islands. But their canoe sailed a northerly course, thereby missing the archipelago. None of the atolls of the Northern Cook and Line Islands fit the description of the sought-after island, so the voyagers sailed on. The ninth island they encountered did have mountains and deep valleys. They called it Nuku Hiva.

Given the inevitable dangers associated with such a long voyage, it is worth asking why the Polynesian people left their rich and fertile homelands in Tonga and

Haatuatua on Nuku Hiva, the Marquesas. In the vicinity of this beach the first Polynesian migrants settled more than 1,500 years ago.

Samoa. Perhaps population pressure played a role, but more likely the answer lies in Polynesian culture and tradition. Though a single cultural entity, the early Polynesians waged war against neighboring islands and communities. The defeated may have had no option but to leave, providing one possible motive for their ventures into the unknown.

Another reason may have been provided by the Polynesian custom of primogeniture. The sons of ruling chiefs did not automatically inherit power a circumstance that possibly motivated them to fit out an expedition and search for an unsettled island. Some historians speculate that curiosity may have played a part as well. After all, the Polynesians were surrounded by a world of water. Among them, as among any group of people, there would have been some who wanted to know what lay beyond the horizon, and who later left to find out.

A small Chilean freighter unloads its cargo off the coast of Easter Island, or Rapa Nui as it is known in Polynesia. Though far easier to reach these days, the island remains one of the most isolated places on the planet.

For one or more of these reasons, the Marquesans moved further east in the second half of the first millennium. With the Marquesas they had reached the end of the relatively closely spaced islands and archipelagoes that extend from Southeast Asia across the Pacific, but they had no way of knowing that. Perhaps they assumed that the chain continued, but it did not.

Even so, Marquesan navigators would have looked for clues before setting out on a long and dangerous journey. There were not many. Little, if any, flotsam reached the Marquesas and if it did, it came mostly from the west, from whence their ancestors had come. But high above migrating birds could be seen heading southeast, an indication that land lay that way. No one knew what kind of land, but it had to exist.

As it turned out, the land did not prove to be much: Rapa Nui, a lone volcanic outcropping of some fifty square miles, nearly two thousand miles directly upwind from Nuku Hiva, and one thousand miles from the nearest inhabited island. No more than a minuscule speck in a vast expanse of ocean, it would have been easy to miss, and yet Marquesan migrants reached it by the seventh century A.D. at the latest. In the history of human migration, this surely represents one of the most amazing chapters.

It took European navigators considerably longer to reach the island. On Easter Sunday, 1722, Dutch navigator Jacob Roggeveen sighted it, and promptly called it Easter Island. Noticing that the islanders would have been hard pressed to build a boat longer than ten feet for lack of wood, Roggeveen dismissed the idea that they had migrated there from some other place. But he had no clue where they had come from. "The ability of human understanding is powerless to comprehend by what means they could have been transported to this island," he later wrote.

As Cook discovered fifty years later, the people of Rapa Nui were related to others in Polynesia, but the canoes they arrived in had long vanished. Subsequent generations had cleared the forests for agriculture, houses, and the vast machinery required to erect their famous statues. As a result, the islanders no longer had the means to navigate anywhere. Once the wood was gone they were trapped and isolated from the rest of the world. And once they were discovered, the theory that they might have come from the west, across thousands of miles of open seas, was rejected as inconceivable.

MIGRATION THEORIES

Of course, the West would not be the West unless it tried to come up with theories to explain how the Polynesians arrived not only on Easter Island, but also on the Marquesas and other islands in the central Pacific. Speculating that God had put them there, as Roggeveen had implied in 1722, no longer worked. There also was no lush southern continent with a few convenient land bridges or, at most, some short crossings that could account for their presence. No, this puzzle was a bit more complicated. It was the type of question Western scientists liked to address.

French navigator Julien Crozet came up with a particularly intriguing idea. After discovering, as Cook had a few year earlier, that the people of New Zealand and Tahiti spoke virtually the same language, and quickly discarding any voyaging link, he suggested that Tahitians and Maoris "were once the same people and inhabited perhaps the same continent, of which the volcanic shocks have left us only the mountains and their savage inhabitants."

Once Crozet's sunken continent idea was discarded, Western scientists grudgingly admitted that these "savage inhabitants" had perhaps made their way there themselves, but the notion of this being a voluntary and controlled migration still seemed a bit far-fetched. During the nineteenth century, for instance, Australian John Lang proposed that the Polynesians had drifted involuntarily to their new homes, much the same way that plant seeds, birds, insects, and other animals had once made their way to every island that dotted the Pacific.

Lang knew that Pacific winds occasionally reversed from their predominantly easterly direction. That, in his view, was the cause of the move east because, on their passage from one island to another, *the unexpected change of wind would often carry the adventurous islanders far beyond their reckoning; and in such circumstances they would either founder at sea, or perish of hunger, or be driven they knew not wither, till they reached some unknown and previously undiscovered island.* According to Lang, once there the "adventurous islanders" would be so busy counting their blessings that the thought of trying to return would hardly come up. Besides, if one of them proffered the idea, the group as a whole was "entirely ignorant as to what course they should steer for their native isle."

A Presbyterian minister, Lang, like a good many of his colleagues, had little confidence in South Pacific know-how. Though his characterization of the inhabitants as ignorant savages became somewhat dated, his theory of accidental drift persisted for a long time. Well into the twentieth century, historians like New Zealander Andrew Sharp contended that it was impossible that Stone Age Polynesians could have intentionally settled the Pacific. Like Lang, he believed the islanders lacked the technology to voyage any great distance in open seas. Short crossings between known islands would have been quite possible, Sharp admitted, but anything more ambitious he discarded as out of the question.

To be fair, some islands in the Pacific probably received their share of accidental arrivals, such as fishermen blown off course or other voyagers caught in adverse winds. But the people who arrived in the Marquesas from Tonga and Samoa, or later in Rapa Nui, carried seedlings and domestic animals with them, not to mention women and children. That hardly classified them as fishermen drifting off-course. Suggesting, as Sharp did, that these people floated blindly around in hopes of landing somewhere implied a rather negative view of Polynesian capabilities. But lacking evidence of strong canoes and precise navigational instruments, many shared this view.

According to early (Western) historians, the Polynesian expansion was the result of accidental drifting by fishermen and mariners. But that contention has been proven invalid. It is now clear that the Polynesian migrations were planned and deliberate.

Even so, the accidental settlement theory had one major weakness: if drift accounted for the Polynesian dispersal, then why did it take place against prevailing winds and currents? Occasionally the winds reversed, and along the equator itself a narrow band of water flowed east, but none of that could explain accidental drifts from west to east.

To some people this was proof that the Polynesians had come not from Asia, but from America. Joaquín Martínez de Zúñiga, a Spanish priest, first proposed this idea in his 1803 book about the history of the Philippines. The theory then lay dormant until the mid-twentieth century, when Norwegian adventurer Thor Heyerdahl and a group of fellow Scandinavians drifted from Peru to the Tuamotu Islands in French Polynesia on a balsa raft. Widely publicized by the media, Heyerdahl's *Kon-Tiki* stunt appealed to the imagination. Before long, the idea of South American settlers crossing the Pacific took root in the popular consciousness, even though it ignored all of the evidence suggesting a move in the opposite direction.

Archaeological research over the past thirty years, much of it undertaken in response to Heyerdahl's claims, has disproved the South American migration theory. The work that uncovered Lapita pottery, along with other archaeological evidence, backs a cultural relationship between Southeast Asia and Polynesia. If there had been an American link, one would have expected to find at least a few arrowheads or some other distinctively South American artifacts, but not a single one has been dug up. Heyerdahl's key argument—that the easterly trade winds would have presented a

SOUTH PACIFIC VESSEL TYPES

Unlike other cultures that learned the art of ships and shipping on the relative safety of protected waters like rivers and lakes, people in the South Pacific had to deal with a different set of conditions. They too made craft from logs, but the waves played havoc with stability. On a lake or river, anyone can paddle a canoe; to stay upright at sea takes experience. When sails were introduced, a dugout became even less stable—a strong gust of wind could easily capsize it; rolling seas made it difficult to right it again.

People in different areas found different solutions to this problem. In the West, people made sure their ships were broad enough to raise a sail without promptly capsizing, and then weighed them down with ballast. In Southeast Asia and the Pacific, people retained their narrow canoes, but either added one or two outriggers, or even another canoe, to obtain the needed stability. Quite different from the Western approach to stability, this represents the solution of a sea-based people.

People in the South Pacific used both types of vessels. The outrigger canoes, usually with a single float, were widely used for fishing and inter-island transport. The double-hulled canoes, in contrast, appear to have been used for the transport of larger numbers of people, either for raiding expeditions or for long-distance voyaging. It is likely that most islands in the Polynesian triangle were discovered and settled with this type of vessel.

For propulsion, the Polynesians appear to have used several types of triangular sails. The early Austronesian voyagers probably used a triangular sail, as did people in Southeast Asia and much later in the seas around India and Arabia. A variant, developed later in the central Pacific, consisted of an apex-down triangular sail. A further development was the uniquely Polynesian claw-shaped (or crab claw) sail type, which probably developed during the first migration from West Polynesia to Central Polynesia some two thousand years ago. Claw-shaped sails taper upward to tips, creating several efficiencies by allowing the wind to escape and reducing the sail area that needs to be supported by the spars. This allows for a lighter construction—less bracing, less weight, and less stress—without reducing sail efficiency. In fact, wind tests have revealed the claw-shaped sail to be one of the most efficient sail designs ever developed.

By the time the Europeans arrived, none of the old voyaging canoes survived, but explorers from Le Maire to Cook observed and drew some of the larger vessels still in use at that time. Though a Western bias occasionally crept in, these drawings have been invaluable in helping to classify some Polynesian vessel types.

Va'a Motu

A medium sized (thirty-three foot) outrigger canoe used throughout the Society Islands (now French Polynesia).

Pahi

Double-hulled Tahitian sailing canoe, twin-masted, approximately fifty to seventy feet long. Caulking was done with fine coconut fiber and adhesive breadfruit sap. Cook called these canoes fit for distant voyaging, and estimated they could cover about one hundred and fifty miles a day. The *pahi* was rigged with Tahitian half-claw sails.

Va'a Alo

A small, planked outrigger canoe from Samoa. Used mostly for fishing, this graceful craft was built from planks sewn together, which were set on a pronounced keel. Along with the smaller dugout or *soatau*, the *va'a alo* was the only native Samoan ship to survive into the twentieth century.

Va'a Ti'i

A ceremonial canoe that was also used for war. In 1774 Cook saw 160 of these canoes and 170 smaller double-hulled sailing canoes carrying "not less than 7,760 men taking off for battle." Given its importance, a *va'a ti'i* could take years to build. Hulls were constructed from carved breadfruit planks built up over dugout keels and assembled with sennit lashings.

Waka Tou'ua

A double-hulled voyaging canoe from the Marquesas. Lacking lagoons and plagued by periods of drought, the Marquesas spawned many voyages in search of new lands. Today no native craft are left, though smaller outrigger canoes survived well into the last century. The last traditional migration voyage dates back at least two hundred years. According to an account recorded by US Navy Captain David Porter, four voyaging canoes left at that time in search of new land, taking sufficient provisions and water, along with hogs, poultry, and seedlings. The small fleet, probably one of the last traditional migration fleets to sail the Pacific, perished.

Tongiaki

Double-hulled canoe from Tonga, with hulls of equal length. Cook measured and drew it during his second voyage to the Pacific. The earliest drawing dates from the Dutch expedition of Schouten and Le Maire (1616). It was built with inserted ribs, like other voyaging canoes. Its underwater lines were identical to those of its Tahitian counterpart.

The Polynesians relied on two principal types of seagoing craft: the outrigger canoe, which could be paddled or sailed, and the double-hulled canoe, which was rigged with a uniquely Polynesian claw-shaped sail.

Camakau
A small single-hulled outrigger used in Fiji. Though they have now mostly disappeared, *camakau* did good service as recently as the oil crisis of the early 1970s.

Baurua
A large ocean-going canoe used in Kiribati, the former Gilbert Islands, in Micronesia.

Ndrua
There is some evidence that the people of Fiji once used double-hulled canoes, but by the 1600s they had developed a different type of vessel called a *ndrua*. It was also double-hulled, but one of the hulls was much smaller and effectively functioned as an outrigger. One *ndrua* was measured at 118 feet in length, accommodating a deck area of fifty feet by twenty-four feet. Its single mast stood more than sixty-five feet high, and supported a large triangular sail.

Kalia
The Tongan version of the ndrua. In Samoa the canoe is known as *'alia*.

Tepuke
A large outrigger canoe, with a distinctive claw-shaped sail, from Taumako in the Reef/Santa Cruz Islands, now part of the Solomons. Some five hundred Polynesians still live on this isolated island, located outside the Polynesian triangle. They built voyaging canoes well into the twentieth century, recently enough for some of the island's elders to recall the techniques involved. Accordingly, Taumako may well be the last island where the knowledge of how to build traditional Polynesian (vis-à-vis Micronesian) canoes survives. Some *tepukes* have recently been reconstructed using traditional materials and methods.

**Polynesian migrants reached Oahu
some 1,500 years ago. Unfortunately,
little is left of the first human presence in Hawaii.**

natural barrier—no longer works either. Not only did Polynesian vessels have some ability to sail upwind, the frequent wind current reversals, especially during El Niño years, would have made the voyages east far more feasible. In fact, like sensible sailors anywhere, Polynesian voyagers would have waited for these wind shifts rather than setting out in the teeth of contrary winds.

Finally, even with favorable winds it would have been difficult to reach isolated islands by accident. Easter Island, for instance, is no more than a speck of land amid a huge expanse of ocean, with no other inhabitable land near it for more than a thousand miles. Computer studies have ruled out accidental drift as an explanation for its settlement. Of course, if plenty of voyaging canoes were set adrift from the Marquesas, there would always be a small chance that one of them, under ideal conditions, could have reached Easter Island. But given the amount of time involved, the chances of its crew still being alive would be minimal. Besides, the Marquesan islanders did not have the luxury of sending out one canoe after another. Though no one knows how many of them left, there probably would have been only a few.

PASSAGES NORTH AND SOUTH

Around the time the Marquesans set out to the east, they apparently also sent one or more voyages north that reached a chain of islands some eighteen hundred miles north by northwest of Nuku Hiva. These voyagers would not have had to beat their way into the wind. In fact, the predominant trade winds would have made it a relatively easy voyage, allowing the canoe to be steered on a broad reach—its optimal sailing angle. Still, that does not explain why the Marquesans left in that direction. Perhaps here too there were flight paths of migratory birds that could be converted into a star compass. Perhaps people were encouraged by visions of fertile islands to the north—no one knows. It was impossible that the early settlers could have known for certain where the land they sought was located.

The earliest archaeological evidence on Hawaii indicates that these first arrivals reached the islands around the middle of the first millennium, settling initially on Oahu and the big island of Hawaii, and later on some of the other islands. The number of people and vessels will never be known with certainty, though it probably was not large. In fact, some anthropologists have suggested that the initial settlement could have resulted from a single voyage. As people increased in number and adjusted to their new environment, they gradually developed their own culture, still with strong links to their island of origin, but with specific adaptations that became uniquely Hawaiian.

This first group of Marquesan settlers had no contact with its region of origin, but it appears that a few hundred years later a new group arrived, this time from the Society Islands. More importantly, this group appears to have maintained some two-way voyaging capability, pulling the Hawaiian Islands at least for some time out of their relative isolation.

Hawaiian legends confirm this link, speaking of a legendary homeland *Kahiki* that was located on Tahiti or Raiatea in the Society Islands. The *Kumulipo*, a long genealogical chant composed in the early eighteenth century, tells of the origin of the Hawaiian islands and traces the royal lineage back to the "time when men came from afar," "afar" generally agreed to mean Kahiki. Converting the genealogies to years led to an arrival date of approximately A.D. 1000, which matches the archaeological record quite well.

At the other end, Tahiti's legends also seem to confirm the voyage, speaking of the widely known Tahitian hero Tafai pulling up not only the islands of the Society

and Tuamotu archipelago, but sailing as far as Hawaii to perform the same feat. Afterwards he returned to Tahiti, the legend continues, only to sail back to Hawaii with a group of settlers. And when the emigrants from the north and their families in the south expressed regret about being separated by such a distance, Tafai linked up the Hawaiian islands to tow them south. Unfortunately this did not work as expected. According to the legend, the rope broke and the islands snapped back, explaining the particular shape of the Hawaiian archipelago.

Much further south, oral tradition also speaks of a legendary homeland of Havaiki, though here the trailblazer is a much more human hero, and his story is told with such consistency that it might have more foundation in fact. It is the story of Kupe, an explorer who reached Aotearoa, the land of the long white cloud, and then returned to tell his people about it. To most of us, Aotearoa is better known as New Zealand.

   Kupe, the legend tells us, had a good reason to sail from Raiatea in a radically different direction. He had killed his cousin Hoturapa, who was married to the woman he loved. Though he claimed the death was accidental, people became suspicious. For Kupe, there was no alternative but to pack his family and belongings onto a canoe and to leave for different shores.

   According to the story, Kupe and his companions sailed for many weeks, growing desperate about ever finding land. But then one day, they sighted it: a land

Aotearoa — the land of the long white cloud — received settlers around A.D. 800, and possibly even earlier. The first migrants probably settled along the northern coast of the North Island.

much larger than the one they knew, with a long white cloud trailing overhead. It took them several weeks to circumnavigate it. From its southern tip they noticed an even larger island to the west. Though it was much colder here than in their homeland, the islands appeared bountiful beyond their wildest dreams. Kupe knew he had a responsibility to return to Havaiki to tell the people there of the discovery.

Legend has it that Kupe succeeded in completing the long return voyage and informing the Raiateans of the great islands far to the south. When some expressed an interest in sailing there, he told them to steer by the setting sun in November. As instructions go, that was not very specific, but Kupe's story was a legend, not a nautical guide. Besides, it proved sufficient to lead the navigator of the great canoe *Kurahau-po* to New Zealand with a new group of settlers.

It is difficult to say how much of this story is true. By converting Maori genealogies to years, it appears Kupe would have traveled around the time of the thirteenth century, though archaeological evidence indicates that the first settlers arrived as much as three hundred to five hundred years earlier. The reason for the departure is plausible, as is the radically different direction. By observing the southwesterly flight path of the long-tailed cuckoo, the Raiateans and Tahitians correctly assumed there would be land in that direction, though they would not have known how far

This islet near Auckland has revealed traces of early human settlement. Its occupants had to contend with very different climatic conditions than the ones they left in the central Pacific.

away it was. New Zealand's earliest archaeological evidence, consisting of fishhooks and adzes, has links with central Polynesia Though most historians do not place too much confidence in mythology, this seems to confirm that the first settlers would have come from the area where Kupe's Raiatea was located, possibly by way of Rarotonga in the Cook Islands. But the trip to Aotearoa would have been a very difficult one. Though the target was huge, there were almost sixteen hundred miles of open sea between Rarotonga and the North Island. As the first voyagers ventured further south, they also ran out of their familiar trade winds, and had to deal with much colder weather.

Maori legends speak of a period of two-way voyaging, describing a number of expeditions in such detail that they resemble historical records. Unfortunately, while details about the selection of crew and canoe and the departure ceremony appear accurate enough, once at sea the voyagers often run into a host of mythological creatures, making it clear that not all of the stories were necessarily based in fact. But a historical base they certainly have. Maori-made (or at least Maori-inspired) artifacts found in French Polynesia and the Cook Islands have confirmed this.

By A.D. 1000 the Polynesians, never more than a million in number, had settled the Pacific from Aotearoa in the south to Rapa Nui in the east and Hawaii in the north—an area so immense that, if placed over Europe and Asia, it would cover the better part of the two. Yet when the first Europeans arrived in the area during the sixteenth century, there was little long-distance voyaging left. The great voyaging canoes had disintegrated; their navigators had long been gone. Pictures of the ships did not exist. If the islanders traveled, it was among neighboring islands, mostly in smaller craft. The only evidence of their daring travels was incorporated in their legends. Though the islanders shared these with Western visitors, they were considered inconceivable, a figment of the islanders' imagination at best.

There are many reasons for the Polynesians' withdrawal from long distance voyaging. First and foremost, by the end of the first millennium their navigators had discovered just about everything there was to be discovered in the Polynesian triangle, and quite possibly far beyond. When the chances of a new expedition finding unsettled land disappeared, the voyagers had less incentive to head out into the unknown. Once the residents of newly settled areas became self-sufficient, they too felt less need to travel. The original settlers might have longed for their homeland, but as they were replaced by new generations, that desire gradually waned. They began to expend their energies on complex religious rituals and monuments instead.

As settlements became more isolated, there were growing suspicions about strangers. Before long that distrust led to the custom of killing newcomers on sight, a practice that was near universal in Polynesia and that discouraged exploratory travel. But the most important reason for the gradual disappearance of long-distance voyaging may have been the fact that the Polynesians did not go to sea for the reasons other cultures did. They sailed to explore and find new islands for settlement. Once a new region had been peopled, there might have been a desire to return to carry news of the discovery and bring along other migrants, but without trade, without commercial motives, there was little reason for continuing intercourse. As a result, the practice died; the canoes rotted away and their navigators vanished. Before long little was left of the great voyages except what could be retained in the minds of men.

SPANISH EXPLORATION

The recorded history of Polynesia begins with the arrival of Europeans, hundreds of years after most of the islanders had stopped long-distance voyaging.

The first European to traverse the region was Magellan, who reached the Pacific in late 1520, after passing through the strait that now bears his name. Unaware of the ocean's extent, he pressed ahead. It took more than three months to cross it, a period that grew into a horrible ordeal. Without sufficient food and water, men succumbed every day. By the end of the crossing, only a few were strong enough to man the vessels.

Given that Magellan and his men were merely trying to survive, they should be forgiven for not making elaborate notes on the islanders. Besides, none of them even met any Polynesians. Magellan managed to cross the Pacific without making landfall until Guam, nearly seven thousand miles from where he left the coast of South America. No wonder one of his chroniclers called the Pacific "so vast that the human mind can scarcely grasp it."

Subsequent Spanish expeditions sailed in Magellan's wake, first to establish a link between the Philippines and Mexico, then to explore the South Pacific. There, the reasoning went, was another continent. Although no one had ever seen it, many believed that it was needed to balance the amount of landmass in the northern hemisphere. And if that were the case, so they reasoned, there was a good chance it might hold some riches as well.

One of the first to sail in search of this southern continent was Alvaro de Mendaña, who set off from Peru with two ships in 1567 and returned two years and seventeen thousand miles later with tales of gold-rich islands far to the west. De Mendaña and his men had run into a group of islands that seemed pleasant enough, though they did not have very welcoming inhabitants. Many of the Spanish were killed in skirmishes, and even more perished on the long and awful return. But people quickly forgot the hardships and how little the expedition had accomplished.

In time, the South Pacific developed into an image of paradise. But exploring it often developed into a grueling ordeal for the first European visitors.

Instead, tales of unlimited riches—of rivers filled with gold and other precious metals—began to circulate. Because the setting reminded European cartographers of King Solomon's mines, the islands became known as the Solomon Islands.

Though de Mendaña wanted to continue exploring the South Pacific, it took him nearly thirty years to win approval for another expedition. This time he was teamed up with Pedro Fernández de Quirós, and given command of four vessels. Aboard were 378 people, among them sailors, soldiers, and a number of prospective settlers, including women and children.

De Mendaña intended to return to the Solomon Islands but sailed too far north and sighted a different group of islands instead. Here he encountered true Polynesians, but it proved to be an unhappy experience for the islanders. Several hundred of them were killed in this, their first encounter with Europeans. In honor of the Viceroy of Lima, de Mendaña called the islands the Las Marquesas de Mendoza, now better known as the Marquesas.

It was here that Pedro Fernández de Quirós made some observations on the islanders' seafaring capabilities, noticing that they did not have "the possibility of sailing to distant parts" for lack of large ships and sailing instruments. When the islanders conveyed that they sailed their canoes to other islands, de Quirós assumed these had to be nearby in view of what struck him as primitive technology. But the closest islands outside the Marquesas archipelago were the Tuamotus several hundred miles south, indicating that the Marquesans still had a voyaging tradition at the time, though it probably would not have been for peaceful purposes.

After leaving the Marquesas, de Mendaña's expedition sailed for weeks without sighting land, until it reached the Santa Cruz Islands, a few hundred miles east of the Solomons. There de Mendaña died of fever, as did nearly a hundred others. De Quirós took over, and decided to make a final attempt for the Solomons, although de Mendaña had been the last person to go there. Unable to locate the islands, de Quirós finally headed for the Philippines and, after provisioning in Manila, set course for Peru. Less than one hundred of the original 378 voyagers survived.

Though the expedition proved a failure, here too the hardships were soon forgotten. De Quirós in particular was eager to get back to the South Pacific, but it took him ten years to win approval. When he set out in late 1605, with three ships and about three hundred men, his goal was nothing less than the mysterious southern continent.

Like previous efforts, the expedition did not achieve its stated goal, though it reached a good many islands unknown to the rest of the world. On his way west, for instance de Quirós sailed through the Tuamotu group and later through the Cook Islands. From there the fleet sailed to Taumako in the Duff Group, northwest of the Santa Cruz Islands. Here de Quirós befriended Tumai, a local chief, who in sign language was able to present a remarkably accurate picture of South Seas geography. The Taumako Islanders still voyaged widely in their outrigger canoes, and Tumai described which islands were small and which large, noting whether the inhabitants were dark or light, and whether they were friendly or not.

The Spanish encountered a well-established culture on the Marquesas. But they could not comprehend how people had ever been able to arrive and settle here.

Acting on Tumai's account of some islands to the south being larger and more lush than Santa Cruz, de Quirós decided to head there instead. Ten days later the fleet reached an archipelago that matched Tumai's description. For some time, the men thought they had finally reached the southern continent, but then it became clear that these too were islands. Even so, de Quirós decided to establish a settlement, calling it Espíritu Santo, one of the first European bases in the South Pacific. But the Spanish did not stay long. Though the land was pleasant and bountiful, a few months later they were at sea again, with de Quirós sailing back to Mexico on a northerly route, and his second in command, Luis Vaes de Torres, heading west between Australia and New Guinea through the strait that was later named for him, and thence north to Manila.

Some of de Quirós's men made notes on the people they met near Espíritu Santo, and included some of the earliest depictions of its inhabitants. They show a Melanesian people, heavily armed with clubs and spears, indicating that the Spanish were not necessarily welcomed in the region. They also mention that the islanders used palm leaves to weave sails, but do not indicate what the canoes looked like. Presumably they were small, for de Quirós never changed his opinion on the seafaring capabilities of the South Seas islanders.

DUTCH DISCOVERIES

The *Roadstead at Batavia*, painted by Adam Willaerts in 1649, now in the Dutch Maritime Museum in Amsterdam. Willaerts never traveled to the East Indies and probably relied on prints and sketches. He clearly conveyed that by the mid-seventeenth century, Batavia had developed into an important port.

Following the expeditions of de Quirós and de Torres, Spain abandoned South Pacific exploration, believing that the chances of finding major new territories were minimal. Furthermore, Spain's resources in the region were needed to counter growing incursions from other European powers.

Holland in particular proved active, using its base at Batavia on Java as a convenient departure point. Just a few months after de Torres sailed through the passage between New Guinea and Australia, a small Dutch ship sailed through its western entrance, and then continued south along Australia's Cape York. Sending parties ashore to check out the area proved dangerous. Several men were killed by the aborigines. "Finding no good to be done there," the voyagers returned to Batavia.

In their search for more efficient sailing routes to the East Indies, the Dutch would chart a great deal more of the South Pacific. In 1615, for instance, two small ships under the command of Jacob Le Maire left Holland to look for a westerly route to the Spice Islands. They sailed around South America, calling its southern tip Cape Horn after their hometown, and then continued north along the Chilean coast. Once the southeasterly trade winds could be picked up, the one remaining vessel set out into the Pacific, reaching first the Tuamotu archipelago and then the Tonga Islands where, as the first European visitors, they were cordially welcomed. The Tongans "showed us much honor and amity," Le Maire later wrote. After taking several weeks to recover from the hardships of the Pacific crossing, the expedition headed north for Batavia.

Meanwhile, Dutch ships outbound from Holland to Batavia around the Cape of Good Hope regularly sighted the west coast of Australia on their southerly route to the east. None of them stopped to examine its seemingly uninviting shores, though that did not prevent the Dutch East Indies Company from claiming the area, calling

it New Holland. When a small expedition was sent south from Batavia in 1622 to explore its northern coast, the voyagers returned with disappointing news. "In our judgment this is the most arid and barren region that could be found anywhere on earth," its leader wrote.

No further exploration of Australia took place until the late 1630s when the Dutch decided to join the search for the southern continent. After a few short exploratory missions, a first major expedition went out in 1642. Headed by Abel Tasman, it was ordered to head south from Mauritius to approximately fifty-two degrees latitude, and then continue along that latitude until it reached land. Tasman did as he was told, but hindered by the extreme cold, decided to head north and continue the search along the forty-fourth parallel instead. It proved a wise decision. If his two ships had stayed further south, they would have encountered no more than a few tiny dots of land at best.

As it turned out, even at this higher latitude a great deal of time passed before the voyagers encountered any land. More than five thousand miles from Mauritius, the crews first sighted it. They sailed along its southern coast and briefly went ashore, noticing that there were signs of human habitation, but nothing of trading interest. Tasman named this area Van Diemen's Land after the governor of Batavia. Later it would be renamed in his honor.

A week after leaving Tasmania, the Dutch navigators discovered another landmass, with mountains towering high into the clouds. Sailing along the shore, they soon encountered people, who paddled towards them in double-hulled canoes. Some

The barren coast of northwest Australia did not receive a flattering description from the first Dutch explorers. Comments ranged from "the most arid and barren region that could be found anywhere on earth" to "an accursed land," as Francisco Pelsaert (see p. 136) wrote.

of them came aboard, and Tasman described them as men of ordinary height, with brown skin and black hair tied in a tuft. But the encounter was not a friendly one. As soon as they saw their chance, the natives killed several Dutchmen in a skirmish, forcing the small fleet to sail on. Elsewhere, too, the natives proved hostile and aggressive.

Tasman and his men were the first Europeans to encounter the Maoris, who had migrated from central Polynesia eight centuries earlier. Though the natives showed no interest in accommodating their Western visitors, Tasman described whatever he could from the vantage of his ship, and even drew some pictures of their canoes for his own journal. They are clearly drawn from a European perspective, with the men shown rowing rather than paddling. Even so, they are among the first pictures anywhere of Polynesian craft and sailors.

Given the unfriendly reception, Tasman and his men never set foot on the "newly discovered" territory. But they claimed it for Holland anyway. It was later named New Zeeland, after one of the provinces of the Netherlands.

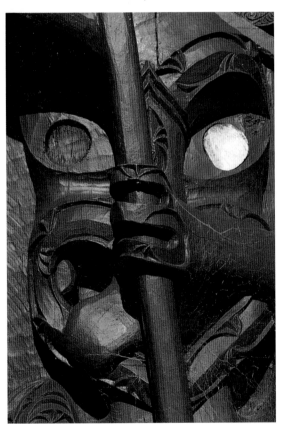

The first encounters between the Maoris and their Western visitors were hostile. European explorers noticed that the various Maori tribes also were seldom on friendly terms.

After leaving New Zealand, Tasman headed north, hoping to find familiar territory. Two weeks later his ships reached Tonga, which Le Maire had visited nearly thirty years earlier. Like his compatriot, Tasman received a warm welcome, with the Tongans eager to provide supplies in return for trinkets. Pleasantly surprised at the "peace and amity" of the island, Tasman recorded his observations, and again made drawings, including some showing outrigger canoes and a double-hulled sailing canoe with sufficient space for shelter and a stone-filled hearth.

From Tonga the ships sailed on, in search of a landmark, because the crews no longer knew exactly where they were. They decided to sail north of the equator and then run along the fourth parallel until they reached the coast of New Guinea. Along the way, they sighted a small group of islands north of the Solomons and a week later reached New Ireland. A few days later the known coast of northern New Guinea came into sight, from whence a course could be set for Batavia.

Since none of the newly found territories seemed to have any commercial potential, officials from the United East Indies Company considered the expedition a failure. As a result, no further voyages were sent from Batavia to explore the South Pacific. The only other Dutch voyage of any consequence for the region left nearly eighty years later from Holland itself. This was the trip that took Jacob Roggeveen around Cape Horn into the expanse of the Pacific and to a chance sighting of Easter Island. The discovery that people were living there puzzled Roggeveen greatly. How they got there, in his view, was beyond "human understanding."

Roggeveen continued on a course west, reaching Samoa, the original Polynesian homeland, ten weeks later. But by then he was no longer interested in speculating about Polynesian origins. What mattered was mere survival. Scurvy was devastating his crew, with several men dying every day. Fortunately, the Samoans nursed Roggeveen and his men back to health. Once revived, they set a course for Batavia, which they reached two months later. But the expedition did not have a happy conclusion. Considered an interloper by the United East Indies Company, Roggeveen was arrested and sent back to Holland a prisoner, bringing an inglorious end to Holland's last major venture into the South Pacific.

FRANCE AND ENGLAND SEARCH THE PACIFIC

Though Holland abandoned its search, the dream of discovering the southern continent grew in stature and importance with every failed attempt. "Who can doubt that such a vast stretch of land when discovered will furnish objects of curiosity and opportunities for profit to equal all that has been produced by America?" wrote French philosopher Charles de Brosses in 1756, voicing the opinion of many of his compatriots. England's main proponent was geographer Alexander Dalrymple, who envisaged a lush continent inhabited by millions, and even went so far as drawing a map of it. *Terra Australis Incognita*, as it became known, was so rich that just the scraps from its table "would be sufficient to maintain the power, dominion, and sovereignty of Britain by employing all its manufacturers and ships," Dalrymple wrote. No wonder many people believed it made sense to go look for it.

In response, both France and Britain fitted out voyages of exploration. Both left in 1766. The British sent two ships, one commanded by Philip Carteret, the other by Samuel Wallis. After the ships proceeded through the Strait of Magellan, a storm separated them. Unable to locate one another, they continued on separate courses.

Carteret's course took him along an uninhabited island he named after one of his midshipmen—Pitcairn Island—and then further north along a series of atolls as far as the Admiralty Islands off New Guinea's north coast. Along the way, he claimed New Ireland for the British Crown before proceeding into known waters and continuing his trip home via the Cape of Good Hope.

Tahiti, with Moorea in the distance. British as well as French explorers felt they had discovered a corner of paradise. Not surprisingly, they regularly returned and used the island as a base for further exploration.

Wallis opted for a more northerly course, which took him through the Tuamotu archipelago and then to one of the most stunning islands yet discovered. The islanders called it Tahiti, and gave the first Europeans to arrive a welcome so warm and friendly that Wallis had trouble keeping his men aboard. Upon his return to England, Wallis gave a glowing report of the reception and the island's strategic value as a base for further exploration, but it was largely ignored. This clearly was not Dalrymple's *Terra Australis*. Wallis's discovery, as a result, was shelved as just one more speck of land with little, if any, commercial value.

Nine months after Wallis, French explorer Louis Antoine de Bougainville arrived in Tahiti as well. De Bougainville was leading France's search for the southern continent, but soon grew enchanted with the island. Tahiti struck him and his crew as nothing less than heaven on earth. Though he found out that other Westerners had been there earlier, he claimed it for France anyway. Nine days later de Bougainville pressed on, convinced he had given his country a corner of paradise. But he knew it would not remain undisturbed. "Farewell happy and wise people," he wrote in his journal. "Remain always as you are."

De Bougainville continued on a westerly course, reaching Samoa and later a group of islands he called the Great Cyclades. These too had been visited by Western ships before. From de Quirós's description, de Bougainville gathered that he was in the vicinity of the Spanish settlement of Espíritu Santo. But unlike the Spanish, de Bougainville did not seek to overpower the natives, writing that he did not wish to be "dishonored for the future by such an abuse of the superiority of our power." He then entered the Coral Sea and sailed as far as Australia's Great Barrier Reef. Before heading back to France via the Cape of Good Hope, de Bougainville also touched upon the Solomons and New Ireland, which had been claimed by Carteret just a few months earlier.

The expedition reached Saint Malo in March of 1769, more than two years after departing. France did well in the process. Aside from obtaining Tahiti, de Bougainville's careful charting helped to establish later claims to French Polynesia. And with new discoveries in the vicinity of New Guinea and the Solomons, the distribution of land in the Pacific became better known. Nothing had been seen of the great southern continent, however, causing de Bougainville to comment that he no longer understood "why our geographers insist that just on the other side of these islands begins a new land." He was only partially right, but it would take another great explorer to finally settle the question.

JAMES COOK

By the time de Bougainville made it back to France, England had already dispatched a new expedition, this one under the command of Navy Lieutenant James Cook, an experienced surveyor and outstanding navigator. The principal purpose of his expedition was to measure the transit of Venus from newly discovered Tahiti. Once that had been completed, Cook was to open his orders and proceed as instructed.

Crammed aboard the former collier *Endeavour*, Cook, his crew, and a complement of scientists and their equipment left Plymouth on August 26, 1768, setting a course for Madeira. From there the ship crossed the Atlantic to Rio de Janeiro and then continued to Cape Horn, which it rounded in late January. Ten weeks later, the *Endeavour* arrived off Tahiti.

POLYNESIAN NAVIGATION

It was not merely the absence of large ships that made early Western explorers doubt Polynesian tales of great voyages. They also did not observe familiar navigational instruments, needed to calculate one's position at sea: astrolabes to measure the height of the sun or a star, for instance, or at least a compass to provide a sense of direction. But some observers noted early on that the Polynesians knew well enough where they were at sea, albeit without the traditional complement of instruments. James Cook always took an interest in indigenous navigation methods, as did Spanish captain José Andía y Varela, who visited Tahiti in 1774, and wrote the following passage in his journal:

'*There are many sailing masters among the people, the term for whom in their language is faatere. They are competent to make long voyages, like that from Otahiti to Oriayatea (Raiatea), which counts for forty or fifty leagues (120-150 miles), and others farther afield. One of them named Puhiuro came to Lima on this occasion in the frigate, and from him and others I was able to find out the method by which they navigate on the high seas. They have no mariner's compass, but divide the horizon into sixteen parts, taking for the cardinal points those at which the sun rises and sets.*

'*When setting out from port the helmsman reckons with the horizon. Thus partitioned counting from East, or the point where the sun rises; he knows the direction in which his destination bears: he sees, also, whether he has the wind aft, or on one or other beam, or on the quarter, or is close-hauled: he knows, further, whether there is a following sea, a head sea, a beam sea, or if it is on the bow or the quarter. He proceeds out of port with a knowledge of these [conditions], heads his vessel according to his calculation, and aided by the signs the sea and wind afford him, does his best to keep steadily on his course.*

'*This task becomes more difficult if the day be cloudy, because of having no mark to count from for dividing out the horizon. Should the night be cloudy as well, they regulate their course by the same signs; and, since the wind is apt to vary in direction more than the swell does, they have their pennants, made of feathers and palmetto bark, to watch its changes by and trim sail, always taking their cue for a knowledge of the course from the indication the sea affords them. When the night is a clear one they steer by the stars; and this is the easiest navigation for them because, there being many stars not only do they note by them the bearings on which the several islands with which they are in touch lie, but also the harbors in them, so that they make straight for the entrance by following the rhumb of the particular star that rises or sets over it; and they hit it off with as much precision as the most expert navigator of civilized nations could achieve.*'

Though much has been written about Polynesian navigation since, José Andía y Varela observed its key elements: a system that relied primarily on celestial information, which was complemented by cues from wind and sea conditions. Unlike Western navigators, who in time obtained instruments and a set of tables to determine latitude based on celestial sightings, and a chronometer to derive a longitude, Polynesian navigators had to memorize a great deal. Of most importance was the star compass, which gave navigators a sense of direction, provided they knew not only the stars needed for navigation, but also where they rose and set throughout the year. On clear days the sun yielded that information, especially at sunrise and sunset; at night the stars did so. When the sun was high in the sky, direction was maintained by observing the direction of the wind and especially that of the sea swell.

Polynesian navigators learned to recognize eight ocean swell systems, which corresponded roughly to the eight octants of a Western compass. The most dominant were the north, northeast, and east swells, created by the strong winter trade winds. As the winter trade winds slackened during spring, swells began to move from the southeast and south. And in late summer and early fall, when winds sometimes blew from the west, then southwest, west, and northwest swells occurred. When winds were constant, the direction of these swells remained steady for weeks and sometimes months on end, enabling skillful navigators to maintain course by keeping a constant angle between their boat and the lines of swells. Sometimes, however, two or three swell systems interacted, and the process of maintaining a correct angle became far more complicated. Navigators then relied on the peaks of the swells as they merged to determine their course.

Today, this ancient form of navigation, called *pukulaw* (wave-tying) in Micronesia, has all but vanished, replaced by Western navigational instruments. But some traditional navigators remain. The most celebrated among them is Mau Piailug, a master navigator from the island of Satawal in the Central Carolines of Micronesia. Mau gained fame in 1976 when he guided *Hokule'a*, a replica of a traditional double-hulled Polynesian voyaging canoe, from Hawaii to Tahiti without charts or navigational instruments. For twenty-five hundred miles, he relied solely on a star compass, based on the rising and setting positions of the stars along the horizon, to determine latitude, and on the ocean swells to maintain direction. At dawn and dusk, he checked the swells' direction against the stars. During overcast nights, when there was no moon to light the swells, he steered the canoe by sensing its pitch and roll in the seaway. It is interesting to note

Hokule'a, as seen on its first voyage to Tahiti. Over the past 25 years, this replica of a double-hulled voyaging canoe has visited all corners of the Polynesian triangle. On each voyage, its crew relied solely on traditional navigation techniques. (courtesy Ed George)

that double-hulled canoes allow for that detection; in or on a single hull this is almost impossible.

Mau made the trip on *Hokule'a* a few more times. Each time, he successfully guided the vessel from one speck in the ocean to another, thousands of miles away, relying on nothing but the stars and the movement of the sea. Along the way he taught Nainoa Thompson, a young Hawaiian, the art of *pukulaw*. Afterwards Nainoa summed up his admiration for Mau's skills: "He knows the waves like he knows an old friend." And like old friends, they "show him the way, no matter how they are covered up."

Since then, several more navigators have been trained in the art of wayfinding, ensuring that the Polynesians' navigation skills won't follow the way of their ships.

Cook stayed in Tahiti for three months, which provided plenty of time to do the required astronomical observations, chart the island, and get to know the Tahitians. Though the reception had been friendly, Cook quickly noticed that Tahiti was not the ideal society his predecessors had made it out to be. There clearly was a very hierarchical order, controlled with near-tyrannical authority by chiefs and priests. The Tahitians also had slaves, and regularly made human sacrifices. War with neighboring islands was a regular affair, involving the deployment of massive fleets of war canoes.

During his stay, Cook made inquiries about Polynesian navigation, befriending Tupuia, a local priest, who provided a wealth of information. Cook quickly discovered that Tupuia had knowledge of many other islands and their sailing distance from Tahiti. From the priest's testimony, Cook drew a map that revealed that the Tahitians had knowledge of all the islands in the central Pacific, from the Marquesas in the northeast to Samoa and Fiji in the west, a distance spanning more than twenty-five hundred miles. Tupuia had visited some of them himself; he knew of others through talks with other navigators, indicating that the Tahitians still made relatively long voyages at the time of Cook's visit.

Tupuia also spoke of native craft, which convinced Cook that Tahitian canoes were able to sail long distances, especially with and across the wind. But the English navigator was not sure about their ability to make efficient progress into the wind, which threw doubt onto his theory of an easterly migration, against the predominant trade winds. Tupuia, however, explained that to sail east the Tahitians simply awaited spells of westerly winds that occurred in late fall and early winter. Assuming the islanders' forebears would also have recognized those seasonal changes, Cook thus envisaged how they might have made it to Tahiti from the western Pacific, and much earlier from Southeast Asia.

When Cook's expedition weighed anchor on July 13, 1769, Tupuia was aboard, guiding the ship to several neighboring islands. Given the proximity of the islands to one another, Cook called them the Society Islands. Next, Tupuia unerringly guided the ship to Rurutu in the Austral Islands, some three hundred miles south of Tahiti. Cook now followed his secret orders, which directed him to sail south to search for *Terra Australis Incognita*, the discovery of which, in the words of the Admiralty "would redound greatly to the honor of this nation as a maritime power, as well as to the dignity of the Crown of Great Britain, and the advancement of the trade and navigation thereof." If nothing had been sighted by the fortieth parallel, he was to proceed west until New Zealand, and chart as much of the country as possible.

Cook did as he was told, and made landfall on the east coast of the North Island, the first European to reach it since Abel Tasman 127 years earlier. Again the Maoris proved hostile, leading to a few skirmishes in which several natives were killed. It depressed the English navigator, for he was desperate to make contact and show he meant no ill will. When a brief parlay could finally be arranged, it immediately became clear that Tupuia and the Maoris spoke more or less the same language, causing Cook to expand the extent of his "great Nation" a first time.

By circumnavigating the country's main islands during his second Pacific voyage, Cook proved that New Zealand was not part of some great southern continent.

The temple of Taputapuatea on Raiatea (French Polynesia)— probably the most sacred place in all of Polynesia. During his stay in the Society Islands, Cook learned a great deal about Polynesian society, which proved far less idyllic than originally imagined. Temples like Taputapuatea were the site of frequent human sacrifice.

Further on, the inhabitants proved somewhat friendlier, enabling the English to collect additional information. With Tupuia as interpreter, Cook and his scientists learned about local culture and customs, many of them strikingly similar to those of Tahiti. His artists sketched the people, their villages, and canoes; and all the while the master navigator mapped the coastline with a care and ability bordering on the incredible. In the course of five months, Cook circumnavigated both the North Island and the South Island, charting twenty-four hundred miles of unknown coast and thereby confirming that New Zealand was not a part of some great southern continent.

Cook had now completed his orders, but rather than sailing back to England, he proceeded to the east coast of Australia, then still known as New Holland, charting the coast from Cape Howe to the northern tip of Cape York—some two thousand miles. Only then did the navigator set a course for home, arriving off the Downs on July 13, 1771.

Exactly one year later Cook was off again, this time with two converted colliers: the *Resolution* and the *Adventure*. The principal purpose of the new expedition was a familiar one: the search for the great southern continent. Although Cook was not sure it even existed, he believed it would be "a great pitty that this thing should not wholly be cleared up." The Admiralty agreed, and sent off its best surveyor with the clear mandate of solving this puzzle once and for all.

Past the Cape of Good Hope much of the trip consisted of sailing as far south as possible in pursuit of a major landmass, but nothing was found. At one point Cook penetrated as near as seventy-five miles from Antarctica, but the ice pack ruled out any additional progress. No one aboard minded that the ships turned north toward warmer climes.

After losing sight of one another in a thick fog, both ships teamed up in New Zealand, and proceeded east for yet another attempt at the southern continent. But with the weather quickly worsening, this proved too difficult. The expedition headed north instead for a familiar anchorage in Tahiti. Once the crews had recovered somewhat, Cook continued on a westerly course, charting and naming several islands in the Cook archipelago and finally arriving off Tonga, which Cook called the Friendly Islands in acknowledgement of the hospitable natives.

With the onset of the southern spring, Cook sailed south again, first to New Zealand and then back into polar waters. Shortly thereafter he lost sight of the *Adventure*. Both ships had again been separated by a storm, and this time there was no opportunity of teaming up again. Cook continued in the *Resolution*, crossing the Antarctic Circle on several occasions. Still there was no land. Surrounded by pack ice in the middle of the southern summer, Cook finally gave up. As far as he was concerned there might be land further south, but "the scraps from its table" would not amount to much. There simply was no way that the land would be habitable, let alone covered with the lush forests and valleys Dalrymple and his colleagues had envisaged.

His main objective achieved, Cook could have headed for home but there was more work to be done. Leaving now, with a strong ship and a good crew at his disposal, would be a terrible waste. There was more of the South Pacific to cover, with "places wholly unexplored" and others "formerly discovered but imperfectly explored." So he headed north again, first to Easter Island. Upon Cook's arrival on March 12, 1774, two islanders paddled out to the vessel and called out for a rope. It immediately struck Cook that they used the same word as the Tahitians. Next one of the islanders climbed aboard and, astonished by the size of the *Resolution*, proceeded

Easter Island's famous *moai* represent a stunning tribute to the islanders' ancestors. But the statues' transport required so much lumber that the island became deforested. Without wood for canoes, the Easter Islanders became totally isolated.

to measure her with outstretched arms, calling out "the numbers by the same name as they do at Tahiti." In Cook's view, there was no doubt that the people of Rapa Nui were Polynesian as well.

From Rapa Nui the ship sailed west, touching upon the Marquesas and Tahiti. There Cook witnessed the departure of a fleet of 300 war canoes, many of them double-hulled and with plenty of room for a crew of warriors and their arsenal. Adorned with flags and streamers, it made for an impressive sight, which was immortalized by William Hodges, the expedition's official artist. The Tahitians also showed Cook the construction of a double-hulled war canoe. He later observed that it had approximately the same length as his own ship.

From Tahiti, Cook proceeded to Tonga, and thence sailed into Melanesia, reaching de Bougainville's Great Cyclades and renaming them New Hebrides. South of the archipelago he found a previously unnoticed island, which quickly proved to be one of the largest discovered thus far. He called it New Caledonia, and spent three weeks charting it. From there Cook sailed back to New Zealand for a major overhaul before setting a course for home.

Cook arrived in England on July 30, 1775, more than three years after leaving. He had gone further south than anyone else, discovered some thirty new islands in his sweeps through the South Pacific, and charted many others. But his most impressive feat was one of negative discovery. At this point it was clear that the concept of a habitable southern continent could no longer be supported.

With the demise of the southern continent theory, explorers lost one of the best reasons for heading to the South Pacific. The great European powers realized that the pickings would be limited to a few atolls or volcanic islands—insufficient reason for outfitting an expedition that could be gone for a couple of years. For that reason, Cook's third and last expedition received a different mandate: to search for the long-imagined Northwest Passage between the Pacific and Atlantic Oceans. A number of people had already examined the possibilities from the Atlantic side, though without success. Cook was asked to do the same from the Pacific.

On July 12, 1776, less than a year after returning from his second voyage, Cook left aboard the *Resolution*, accompanied this time by the *Discovery*. After a passage around the Cape of Good Hope, both ships arrived in New Zealand in February of the following year. From there the voyage continued north to Tonga, where Cook spent nearly three months, charting, observing, and provisioning. In July the fleet sailed on to Tahiti, where it received the typically warm welcome. This time Cook stayed nearly four months—longer than any European before, which enabled him and his scientists to find out even more about the islanders. In early December he sailed on, setting a course for the North American coast, in search of a northwest passage.

Three weeks later, after sailing about a thousand miles, he sighted a small, uninhabited island. As it was Christmas Eve, he called it Christmas Island, a name it bears to this day. Another three weeks later, the two ships came across a more substantial group of large, mountainous islands. None of them were marked on Cook's chart. No European had ever seen them.

Some natives paddled out to the ship, astonishing Cook and his crew by speaking a language similar to the one heard throughout the South Pacific. An even greater surprise awaited him when he went ashore on the island of Kauai. Assuming that Cook was a great god, people prostrated themselves wherever he passed. The English commander was puzzled, but surmised it was the way the islanders showed deference to their chiefs.

Cook was told of even larger islands not far to the east, but he was eager to begin his search for the Northwest Passage. Accordingly he left after just two weeks, though he made up his mind to return, speculating that his chance discovery might prove "the most important that had hitherto been made by Europeans throughout the extent of the Pacific Ocean." He named the islands after the Earl of Sandwich, who headed the Admiralty at the time. Later they would be renamed after the largest island in the group: Hawaii.

For much of 1777, Cook explored the northwest American coast, sailing as far as the Bering Strait and the polar circle, before the pack ice turned him back. This too proved an exercise in negative discovery. Just as there had been no fabulous southern continent, a practicable northwest passage proved a figment of the imagination of non-sailing geographers. In late summer Cook turned back, intending to return a year later to investigate whether there was perhaps another route along the Siberian coast.

Like the generations that would follow him, Cook thought the prospect of wintering in Hawaii more appealing than staying in northern regions, so he ordered the two ships on a course south. In late December they arrived off the island of Hawaii— the largest of its group. Here too the inhabitants were deferential, honoring Cook as the great god Lono who had left long ago but had been expected to return with all kinds of wonderful gifts. Cook clearly qualified: his imposing ships looked like the sort of vessel a god would use, and the nails, knives, and other things the English traded for provisions certainly qualified as unique and wonderful. Like other Polynesians, the Hawaiians had never seen or used metals.

Cook did not know this, but accepted the accolades with grace. While the battered *Resolution* was being repaired, he toured the island, attending dancing and wrestling exhibitions, and making notes on the people. One of his officers marveled at how young Hawaiians used boards to ride waves "with an incredible swiftness." Cook and his officers also noticed the Hawaiians' strong double-hulled sailing canoes, but communication proved difficult if not impossible. There was no Tupuia or other interpreter here to provide Cook with answers to his questions. His experience compelled him to compose his famous question: "How shall we account for this Nation spreading itself so far over this vast ocean?"

Unfortunately, Cook never had a chance to answer that question from his own perspective. A few days later he was killed in a skirmish. Both sides were stunned: the English because they had lost their commander; the Hawaiians because their god had been killed. Cook's body was cut up, the flesh burned or perhaps eaten, but the bones were preserved and returned to the ship by a priest. Even then, the Hawaiians wanted to know when Lono would return, unable to accept that Cook was gone forever.

With James Cook, the Polynesians lost the one man who could have validated their seafaring exploits. After all, Cook was a great navigator himself, who knew the difficulties of sailing the Pacific firsthand. He was interested in their navigational techniques, constantly trying to understand how the Polynesians had settled throughout the expanse of the Pacific. He was the first Westerner, probably the first person ever, to visit the three corners of the Polynesian triangle and all the main island groups in between and, most important, he did so at the onset of the European contact. What Cook saw in Hawaii, Rapa Nui, and Aotearoa was still unaffected by Western influences. It would not stay that way for long.

Subsequent historians had much less to work with. Within years, Polynesian societies began to undergo tremendous changes, eroding island traditions. The few voyaging canoes that remained disappeared; traditional navigational knowledge

In the end, little remained of the great voyagers but their legends and temples. And these too were subject to Western interpretation.

gradually vanished. There were still tales of ancient navigators like Tafai and Kupe, but they soon began to incorporate new elements: some because the islanders discovered geographical information that had been unknown or long forgotten, others because they were recorded by Western anthropologists eager to prove a point. The story of Polynesian seafaring became one of extremes, one side assuming that the Pacific had been populated by people who accidentally settled it, the other proclaiming that it was peopled by a race of supernavigators, who crisscrossed the Pacific "as western peoples explored a lake."

As always, the truth lies somewhere in between…

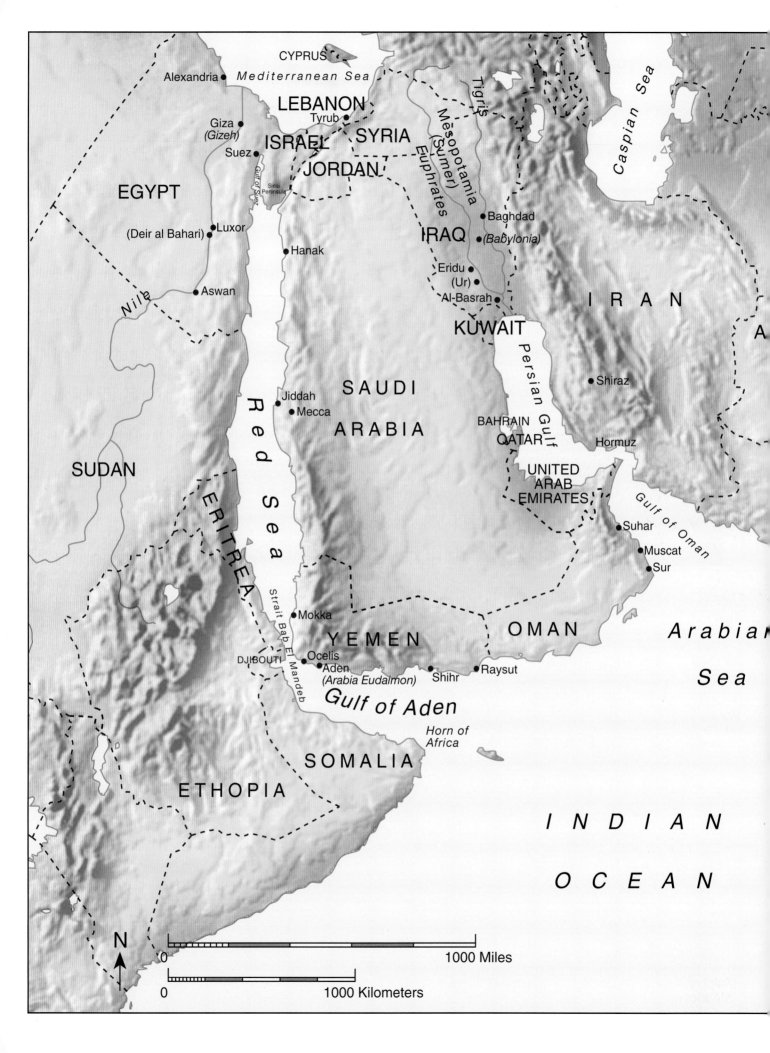

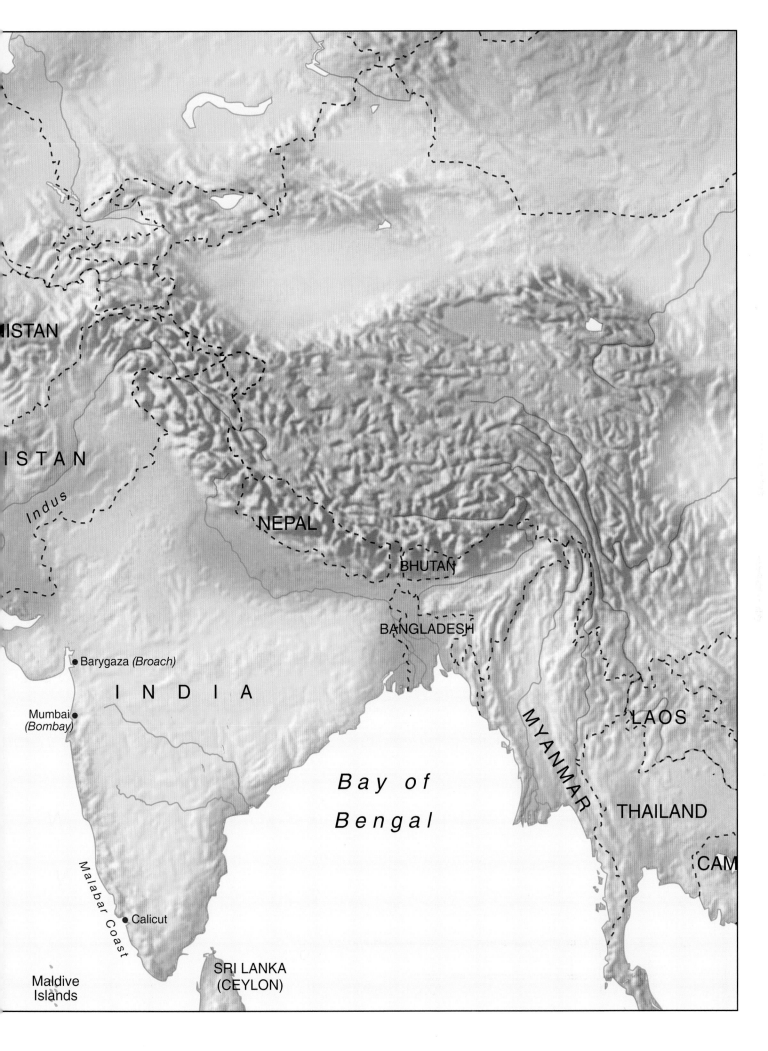

SONS OF SINBAD

'In a bay on the left side of this gulf, there is a market town called Muza, about twelve thousand stadia from Berenice for those sailing southward. The entire place is crowded with Arab shipowners and seafaring men, and is busy with the affairs of commerce; for they carry on a trade with the far-side coast and with Barygaza, sending their own ships there.'

This brief passage comes from one of the earliest guidebooks for traders and sailors—the *Periplus of the Erythraean Sea*, written some time during the first century A.D. Named after Erythras and his mythical tribe of red men, the Erythraean Sea is now better known as the Red Sea. But the *Periplus* describes it as extending far beyond, past the Strait of Bāb El-mandeb into the Gulf of Aden and onward to India, covering the entire Indian Ocean as then known to Western traders.

We do not know much about the author of the *Periplus*, other than that he lived in Alexandria. A trader, he probably visited a number of places along the ancient sea route to the East, all of which he described with a quick eye. But his work contains more than information about places and people. The *Periplus* also contains the first notes on the seafaring habits of the people who lived along the shores of the Arabian peninsula.

Another seven hundred years would pass before Arab seafarers set off to leave their indelible mark on the history of ships and shipping, but the *Periplus* implies that their ancestors were capable sailors as well. Living astride two of the greatest and busiest sea routes of the ancient world—the Red Sea and the Persian Gulf—they probably had no choice. They had to go to sea to survive. Though they did so hesitantly at first, they eventually learned to master the sea. In the process, they shaped the course of maritime history, and thus of the world.

THE FIRST RIVERINE TRADE

Southern Iraq is a desolate land of windswept hills and deserts. There is little to remind us that this was once the fertile plain between the Tigris and Euphrates rivers known as Sumer—hardly anything to indicate that this area saw the birth of a major civilization. There are no cities or temples and only a few ruins. What remains is covered by tells, created by thousands of years of sand and neglect. Rising above the monotonous landscape, they pinpoint the location of long forgotten cities like Ur, Erech, and Eridu.

The view is deceptive. More than six thousand years ago, these were thriving communities, bursting with vitality. They were among the earliest centers of organized trade and commerce. Their people invented and developed a means of recording their transactions, bringing about a revolution in communication. Here art, technology, and political life—fundamental to the concept of civilization—found room to grow and expand.

Transporting people and their goods, the Sumerians quickly grasped that even the most primitive raft could carry far more than a mule or a cart. Boats also did not need roads; all they required was water—a river, a ditch, or even a stretch of swamp. Accordingly it was here, on the great rivers and the many irrigation canals that crisscrossed the plain, that the world's earliest riverine trade developed. Unfortunately, little is left to show us what it looked like. Sumer's boats and rafts, fashioned out of reeds or hides, have long vanished. The rivers have changed their course, abandoning the cities they once connected. Even the coast has receded. The remains of Eridu, once a busy seaport, now lie far inland, pushed away from the coast by relentless siltation.

When the river moved, so did the people. Without it they were deprived not only of the water that irrigated their fields but also of their principal highway. They went north, or moved along with the course of the river. Before long Sumer began to lose its importance. The balance of power and wealth shifted further north instead.

During the third and second millennia B.C., the northern reaches of Mesopotamia, known as Babylonia, became very powerful. Babylonian merchants traded throughout the ancient Near East, and with places known as Dilmun, Magan, and Meluhha. Dilmun was located on the island of Bahrain, then—as now—an important trading center. Magan was in all likelihood located in Oman, and exported timber, copper, and other raw materials. Meluhha, on the other hand, lay on the other side of the Persian Gulf, possibly as far away as the Indus Valley. There was no way of reaching these areas except by sea, confirming that maritime trade was well organized by that time.

The little we know about the vessels that sailed these waters comes mostly from the cylinder seals merchants used to personalize their documents. Most people chose mythological symbols, but occasionally merchants would pick a topic relating to their work, showing a ship or some cargo. Small as they are, the imprints do not show much detail, but they confirm that boats and rafts were a common part of Mesopotamian business life.

The *Standard of Ur*, currently on exhibit in the British Museum, provides a rare glimpse of daily life in Sumer.

Inscribed on clay tablets, Mesopotamian records provide insight as well, noting the size of a ship's crew or the costs involved in chartering it. One tablet, discovered at Ur, lists the materials needed to construct boats, from timber pitch for the hulls to caulking materials and hides. But by far the most intriguing nautical artifact from this era is a small, clay model of a boat, found in a grave at Eridu. What makes the 5,500-year-old model so interesting is a vertical socket, placed in the middle. Some historians believe it was a mast step, and the holes in the gunwale, possibly inserted there to fasten the rigging, seem to confirm this. Though we cannot be certain, this simple model may represent the oldest known sailing vessel. It demonstrates that the people of Mesopotamia, in addition to their cultural legacy, left a profound mark on the maritime doings of the ancient world.

ANCIENT EGYPT

West of the Tigris and Euphrates was the Nile, which formed a natural highway for ancient Egypt's trade and commerce. Rock and pottery carvings, some dating back some six thousand years, show long and narrow craft, assembled from bundles of papyrus and propelled by men paddling along the sides. These boats were plying the Nile when Pharaoh Menes, according to legend, became the first ruler of Egypt.

During the fourth millennium B.C., ships with sails appeared on the Nile. They were constructed of papyrus as well, on which a bipod mast with a square sail was set. The split mast structure was needed to spread the weight over the fragile hull. To sail south, to Upper Egypt, the ships ran before the prevailing northerly winds. On the way back they relied on rowers or paddlers, their task made easier by the current.

For nearly a thousand years, these vessels changed little in appearance, but then an important development took place. Shipbuilders began using wood rather than papyrus, enabling them to construct a hull that could keep people and cargo relatively dry. Wood was scarce in Egypt, so most of it had to be imported but it proved worth the effort. For one thing, wooden boats could carry considerably more cargo, which shipowners and merchants would have appreciated. For another, wooden ships were no longer confined to the relative calm of rivers. With these vessels people could venture into the open sea, in search of new trade and new ideas.

The Nile in Aswan. The ancient Egyptians learned the art of shipping on the river, which developed into their principal highway for commerce.

From the third millennium B.C. onward, the Egyptians began building ships that ventured far into the Mediterranean. An expedition to Byblos in present-day Lebanon, for instance, set out during the reign of Pharaoh Snefru more than five thousand years ago. It returned with a cargo of wood, needed for the construction of temples, palaces, and ships. Other voyages went to Crete and Syria, and further north to obtain pinewood and resin. Overland trade routes reached Egypt from the Sinai peninsula with copper and turquoise, and from the mythic land of Punt, much further south, which exported highly prized incenses like myrrh and frankincense.

Passing as it did through many hands, overland trade was expensive. To lower the cost, the Egyptians sought alternatives. They decided to develop a sea route to Punt, now believed to have been located in the Horn of Africa, along the north coast of Somalia. First they constructed a canal, linking the Nile with the Red Sea, but it proved too difficult to maintain and soon fell into disrepair. Instead, they decided to operate the sea route to Punt from the head of the Red Sea, near present-day Suez.

Even then the venture required a formidable effort. First wood and resin for the ships had to be imported from Lebanon, transported down the Nile, and carried across 150 miles of desert to the head of the Gulf of Suez. Once assembled, the vessels began the long and dangerous journey down the entire length of the Red Sea.

For hundreds of miles the ships passed along a barren coast. If bad weather threatened there were few, if any, refuges. Much of the route was affected by unpredictable crosscurrents and flanked by coral reefs, stretching far into the sea. Avoiding these demanded knowledge of their extent, as well as navigational skill. Once the ships made it to the southern end of the Red Sea, they sailed through the strait of Bāb El-mandeb into the Gulf of Aden, and onward to the Horn of Africa.

The voyages to Punt generally took two years. For the first part of the trip the vessels made good progress, taking advantage of the stable north winds that blow from the Gulf of Suez as far as the central Red Sea. Once there the winds reversed, however, making progress slow and arduous at best. Rowers then became essential. The return trip was more or less the same: first a smooth sail with southerly winds and then the long passage north, tacking back and forth or rowing against fierce north winds.

Despite these hardships and the very real dangers of being wrecked or attacked by pirates, the Egyptians regularly sent fleets to Punt for more than a thousand years. The first recorded trip left during the reign of Pharaoh Sahure, nearly forty-five hundred years ago. But the most detailed expedition dates to about a thousand years later, to the reign of Queen Hatshepsut, who sent five ships to Punt around 1495 B.C.

A series of colored reliefs immortalize the expedition in Hatshepsut's temple at Deir al Bahri, across the Nile from Luxor. The first illustrated account of a trading voyage, they tell us much about the ships and their crews, as well as the trade itself. Accompanied by detailed descriptions, the reliefs show how the Egyptians were received in Punt and how they returned, their ships deeply loaded with riches: *"all goodly flagrant woods of God's Land, heaps of myrrh-resin, with fresh myrrh trees, with ebony and pure ivory, with green gold of Emu, with cinnamon wood, khesyt wood, with ishmut incense, sonter-incense, with apes, monkeys, dogs, and with the skins of the southern panther, with natives and their children."* *"Never,"* so the inscription continues, *"was the like brought back to any monarch since the world began."*

Judging from the reliefs, the ships were about one hundred feet long, with fifteen rowers on each side and two men to control the side rudders. The depictions also clearly show one of the key characteristics of Egyptian ships: a massive cable, which ran from stem to stern. A remnant from the days of papyrus-built ships, the cable could be twisted amidships to strengthen the hull and prevent the ends from sagging. Each ship had one mast, which supported a broad square sail and yards consisting of two spars lashed together. Though relatively primitive, the rigging configuration

The temple of Queen Hatshepsut at Deir al Bahri, across the Nile from Luxor (left). On its walls, an illustrated account of the voyage to Punt was carved. Though the colored reliefs are fading, they still provide a superb view of what the expedition entailed.

would have allowed the sail to be braced round to the wind, enabling the ships to sail with more than just a following wind.

These were the best ships ancient Egypt ever produced, and they completed remarkable voyages. But not long after Hatshepsut's reign, interest in these expeditions began to erode. Never a maritime power in the first place, Egypt preferred to leave sea trading to others. From the middle of the second millennium B.C. its merchant fleet began to decline. Not long thereafter so did its power and influence.

THE PHOENICIAN MARITIME ENTERPRISE

It did not take long for others to fill the void left by the Egyptians' departure. To the north, the people of Minos, on the island of Crete, began to control much of the Mediterranean's trade, though it was probably carried on ships from the surrounding Aegean islands. Following the decline of Minoan civilization (see Chapter 4), the skilled mariners of the eastern Mediterranean seaboard stepped in. The Greeks called them *Phoinikis*—the purple people—after a highly prized red dye they produced from sea snails. To us they are better known as the Phoenicians.

Phoenicia's greatest maritime achievement was the opening of the western Mediterranean. From about 1000 B.C., Phoenician mariners ventured west from their strategically located ports in today's Lebanon, establishing trading posts in

EGYPTIAN BOAT MODELS

The ancient Egyptians believed in a primeval watery mass from which heaven and earth were created. According to their mythology the Nile sprang from this watery chaos and was divided into two rivers: one across the land, the other across the heavens. The sun, the moon, and the stars sailed in reed floats on the celestial Nile each day, explaining the sun god's journey around the heavens. Once beyond the horizon, the sun continued its trip on a nocturnal Nile under the world, accounting for its reappearance on the other side each morning.

This celestial Nile figured prominently in the Egyptians' beliefs about the afterlife. In fact, they assumed the deceased had to sail it to reach the hereafter—a fortunate circumstance for maritime history because it caused ships to play an important role in funerary rites. Their inclusion in burial sites dates back to Egyptian prehistory, with some 5,500-year-old graves including pots painted with boats. The oldest known Egyptian tomb painting also has a boat procession as its principal theme. Though the boats look similar to the ones painted on decorated pots, the painting is now so faded that it is difficult to interpret.

The development of decipherable writing made it easier to figure out the religious significance of the many boats found in tomb paintings. But more importantly, by the First Dynasty the practice of burying actual boats with the dead began. Given the assumption that the deceased and their belongings would have to travel over water, a full-scale boat was believed to be the best option. Since most people could not afford that, they used boat models, a custom that continued for several thousand years. Though innumerable models are of a symbolic nature, many were built with a remarkable eye for detail, providing a unique visual overview of Egyptian ships and shipping throughout dynastic times.

The pharaohs often had entire fleets of boat models buried with them, in addition to full-sized ships. In some cases the ships were actual boats, which had probably sailed prior to being buried; in others, large funeral ships were included, which would not have done too well sailing the earthly Nile. The most impressive of these were constructed for Khufu (known to the ancient Greeks and most of the Western world as Cheops), the builder of the Great Pyramid at Giza. They joined him in disassembled form at his final resting place.

Actually, several funeral boats were originally buried near the Great Pyramid; all but two were removed in antiquity. Of these two, one was excavated in 1954 and brilliantly reassembled over the next several years by Egyptian conservator Hag Ahmed Moustafa. The other still lies in the pit where it was placed more than forty-five hundred years ago. Tests have already confirmed its condition to be inferior to that of the first.

What emerged under Moustafa's guidance is a veritable masterpiece of Egyptian shipbuilding: an elegant funerary ship some one hundred forty feet long and twenty feet wide. Some twelve hundred pieces had to be assembled, a process that shed considerable light on ancient shipbuilding. The planks of the ship were held together by tenons: these were flat tongues of wood designed to fit into edge cuttings called mortises. Relatively small, they served mostly to maintain the vessel's shape. To actually hold the planks together and provide structural strength, the shipbuilders used lashings. The mortise-and-tenon technique was in all likelihood an Egyptian invention that, with some modifications, spread throughout the ancient world.

There is still some uncertainty over the exact function of the ship. Some historians believe that it was a solar ship, designed to take the deceased pharaoh on his journey through heaven. Others believe it was one of the actual vessels that took Khufu to his tomb during the funeral. And still others maintain that it was one of several official vessels that pharaohs would have used on ceremonial occasions.

All of these scenarios are possible, individually or even jointly, provided the vessel, if actually afloat, was used on very calm waters. But one thing is certain. This, the oldest wooden ship in the world, displays a level of skill and ingenuity that rivals the monuments next to which it was buried.

The Cheops ship, displayed in the Solar Ship Museum next to the Great Pyramid at Giza, is the oldest wooden ship in the world.

The Cape of Good Hope. Convention tells us it was first rounded by the Portuguese in the late 15th century, but the Phoenicians possibly preceded them by 2,000 years.

Sardinia, Ibiza, and along the North African coast. Eventually they sailed through the Strait of Gibraltar, and founded the city of Tartessos near present-day Cadiz, where they stockpiled silver from local mines as well as tin, brought there from the north. One of the ingredients of bronze, tin was always in short supply in the eastern Mediterranean. Its trade made Phoenician traders a fortune.

But the Phoenicians did not confine their activities to the Mediterranean. Following the decline of Egypt's sea power, they also became involved in the trade of the Red Sea, enlisted by the rulers of the region. There are references in the Bible to the ships of King Solomon sailing as far as Ophir in India to obtain gold, silver, and a variety of exotic products. Solomon's vessels, the Biblical account continues, were manned by Phoenicians, sent by King Hiram of Tyre. Though the voyage reportedly was made only once every three years, it established the Red Sea as a sea route to the riches of the East as early as 1000 B.C.

If Phoenician sailors ventured down the Red Sea and into the Indian Ocean, one might assume they also went south along the East African coast. There is uncertainty about this, though the Greek historian Herodotus mentions a Phoenician fleet that left the Red Sea some time around 600 B.C., supposedly to look for a southern sea route between the Red Sea and the Mediterranean.

According to the great historian, writing some one hundred fifty years later, the fleet boldly sailed into "the great southern sea," halting once a year for a couple of months to plant crops and gather a harvest before continuing onward. Three years

later it returned via the Strait of Gibraltar and the Mediterranean—the first, it appears, to have circumnavigated the entire African continent.

But Herodotus was not convinced, writing that "they reported a thing which I cannot believe, but another man may, namely that in sailing around Libya [that is, Africa] they had the sun on their right hand." Herodotus was puzzled because he assumed that any ship sailing west in the northern hemisphere would always have the sun to the south, and thus to its left. He did not realize that a ship going far enough south of the equator would have the sun to the north, and hence to its right. Herodotus's doubt thus seems to confirm that the expedition actually succeeded, though modern historians are somewhat skeptical too. Nonetheless, if any sailors in antiquity ever set out to round Africa, it would have been the Phoenicians who stood the best chance of returning to tell the story.

Unlike the Egyptians and, much later, their Greek competitors, the Phoenicians left few written or visual chronicles. They were businessmen first and foremost, far more interested in short-term profits than long-term recognition. They were even known to spread falsehoods to discourage others from venturing where they went.

Although the Phoenicians were not the first or last to do so, it means we know relatively little about the ships they used on their trade routes. Fortunately there are a few illustrations that show the vessels used for trading with the West—the Tarshish ships as they were called—presumably because they went as far as Tartessos. The illustrations show big, sturdy vessels, capable of carrying considerable quantities of cargo. Equipped with a single square sail, they do not seem to have provided for rowers, indicating that these were among the first vessels used exclusively for sailing. For several hundred years, they played a major role in the long-distance trade of the Mediterranean, and possibly of the Red Sea as well.

Even so, the Phoenicians' commercial reign would not last. From the eighth century B.C. onward, they began to be confronted by the Assyrians, who were moving west to obtain a Mediterranean base. A nation of traders and sailors, Phoenicia was no

A Phoenician galley, shown in a relief from the palace of the Assyrian king Sennacherib, ca. 700 B.C. It demonstrates that the Phoenicians did more than carry trade at sea; they also had the capability of protecting it.

match for Assyria's well-trained armies, and one by one its ports were overwhelmed. Tyre, the last remaining stronghold, fell in 666 B.C. Mourning the fall of Phoenicia's proudest city, the prophet Ezekiel compared its fate to the demise of a ship, inadvertently leaving us one of the few descriptions of Phoenician shipbuilding:

> 'Cyprus from Senir they used
> for your planking.
> They took a cedar from Lebanon
> to make you a mast.
> From the tallest oaks of Bashan
> they made your oars.
> They built you a deck of cedar
> inlaid with ivory from Kittim.
> Embroidered linen from Egypt was used
> for your sail and your flag.
> Purple and scarlet from Elishah
> formed your deck tent.
> Men from Sidon and from Arvan
> were your oarsmen.
> Your sages, Tyre, were aboard
> serving as sailors.
> The elders and craftsmen of Gebal
> were there to caulk your seams.'

The fall of Tyre brought an end to Phoenicia's domination of the eastern Mediterranean. But its maritime legacy endured for many years to come, as Phoenician mariners sailed the Red Sea and beyond. Others established themselves further west, founding colonies in Sardinia and along the North African coast. From there they played a major role in the sea trade of the western Mediterranean, until the Romans defeated them during the second century B.C.

A WESTERN PRESENCE

Little is known of the sea trade of the Near East from the fall of Tyre until the unification of Western Asia and Egypt by Darius the Great (521 - 485 B.C.). The Persian emperor, who understood the importance of linking the corners of his empire by land and by sea, is known to have sent a fleet from the Indus around the Arabian peninsula to Egypt. He also ordered the reconstruction of the old canal linking the Nile and the Gulf of Suez—a huge effort that cost thousands of lives. To prove its usefulness Darius sent a fleet from the Nile through the canal to the Red Sea and on to Persia, but before long this man-made waterway once more fell into disrepair.

Persia's attempts to control the eastern Mediterranean met with failure at the battle of Salamis in 480 B.C. Instead, it was the victorious Greeks who eventually took over Phoenician trade routes, colonizing and controlling the Mediterranean coast from Massalia (Marseilles) to the Black Sea. Under Alexander the Great (356 - 323 B.C.) they also expanded far to the east, reaching the Indus Valley—then still the limit of the world known to the West.

Towards the end of his short life, Alexander relied on Phoenician shipbuilders and sailors to explore the Persian Gulf and colonize its shores. Ships were brought in parts from the Mediterranean coast to Mesopotamia and reassembled at the head of

the Gulf. There is mention of some vessels reaching Dilmun, today's Bahrain, but none seem to have passed beyond Hormuz into the Arabian Sea. As a result, the sea route to India via the Persian Gulf remained largely unused. To obtain Eastern goods, the ancient Greeks relied on the overland caravan routes through Persia instead.

Alexander also sent a fleet from Egypt down the Red Sea to round the Arabian peninsula, but it turned back as well, after reaching the Strait of Bāb El-mandeb. For the next several hundred years, the Red Sea remained under the control of the Egyptians and coastal Arabs, gradually losing its former function as the sea route to India.

Control over the trade between East and West shifted south instead. Greek records speak of the Sabaeans and Minaeans of South Arabia ruling the trade between Europe and Asia during much of the third and second centuries B.C. Though they refer mostly to the overland caravan trade, these accounts also mention that there were Minaean ships that regularly sailed for the Red Sea. Other South Arabian ports and towns also benefited from the trade between India and Egypt, developing into provisioning ports for the ships linking East and West.

Along the Persian Gulf coast the people of Gerrha were the most active merchants. They acted as middlemen in the trade between South Arabia and Persia—a trade serviced by land and by sea that made them a fortune. Unfortunately, we know next to nothing about the ships that were used to make the voyages from the South

Alexandria was the meeting point between East and West in antiquity. But little is left of its former role.

Arabian coast into the Persian Gulf or the Red Sea. Presumably the hulls were sewn, but nothing is known about the sails, rigging, or hull shape. Nautical archaeologists still hope to find a shipwreck from those times, but the lack of rivers on the Arabian peninsula and the exposed nature of its coast have left few, if any, pickings.

Not until 120 B.C. was the Red Sea route put to regular use again, reportedly by a certain Eudoxus of Cyzicus, who led several expeditions by sea from Egypt to India. A Greek seafarer named Hippalus, who accompanied one of these voyages, later gained immortality by figuring out how to sail directly from the south Arabian coast to India using the southwest monsoon. Though it made for a somewhat rougher passage, the new route shortened dramatically the duration of a trip to India, bringing its riches within easier reach. Other Greeks, and later the Romans, followed his course, improved on the routes he recommended, and continued to reach India this way for several hundred years.

Once these trips began to take place with some frequency during the onset of the Christian era, more information on the area became available. By far the most important document remains the *Periplus of the Erythraean Sea*, compiled by a Greek merchant living in Alexandria—at that time the western terminal of the sea route to India.

The *Periplus* contains a wealth of information, not only about the ports and trade products of the region, but also about their political, historical, and economic importance. Like any good nautical guide, it includes sailing directions and descriptions of coastal features, presented in such detail that the writer probably had firsthand experience of these places. There are also descriptions of places he did not visit, like the Indian coast south of Bombay and the East African coast, presumably collected from sailors and traders who had ventured that way.

The remnants of a Sabaean temple in Marib, Yemen. This was once the seat of the legendary Queen of Sheba, whose territory benefited from the caravan trade between East and West.

Naturally the *Periplus* becomes vaguer as it ventures farther from home, describing the area beyond the Ganges River as difficult to reach because of its "great cold" and "some divine influence of the gods." But up to the area of the Indian West Coast it is generally accurate and, though a good number of towns have since vanished, its descriptions can be followed on a modern map. Then again, the *Periplus* was written for and by traders. Unlike the work of classical historians, which was often compiled hundreds of years after the fact, it contained practical and up-to-date information, providing us with a fascinating look at the world of ships and shipping around the beginning of the Christian era.

Pliny the Elder's *Natural History*, published around A.D. 77, complements the *Periplus*, containing much interesting information on Rome's trade with India, among a wealth of other topics. From it we learn, for instance, that wine, bronze, gold, and a variety of manufactured articles were loaded aboard ships in Alexandria, and then carried down the Nile as far as Coptus, some twenty-five miles north of Luxor. From there the cargo was shipped overland to the Red Sea ports of Berenice and Myus Hormus and transferred to large vessels for the trip around the Arabian peninsula.

Ships continuing on to India provisioned at Ocelis near the tip of southwestern Arabia or at Cane, also known as Qana, further along the coast. From there they cut straight across the Arabian Sea to the Indian Malabar coast, where they traded jewels and spices. Some ships sailed to northern India, following the South Arabian coast as far as Cape Syagrus in western Oman before heading for Barygaza (Broach) and other ports north of Mumbai (Bombay). Western goods were traded here for silk, spices, cotton, and other fine cloths.

THE COASTAL ARABS

Pliny's *Natural History* and the *Periplus of the Erythraean Sea* show that there was a considerable traffic between East and West via the Red Sea, with Egyptian, Greek, Roman, and presumably local ships regularly making the long trip to India. Although the sailings were occasionally interrupted by political instability, it was never for long. In fact, by the first century these voyages took place with remarkable frequency. The Greek geographer Strabo, for instance, observed that no less than 120 ships sailed from Myus Hormus along Egypt's Red Sea coast to India every year to supply the West's growing demand for oriental luxuries.

Both books also are the first to shed a bit of light on the seafarers of the Arabian peninsula. Surrounded by water on three sides, the peninsula's long coastlines included some of the most fertile areas of Arabia, regions where people were likely to settle and thus take to the water. Along its western and eastern side, these coastal Arabs were within short sailing distance of the two most important centers of ancient civilization: Egypt, across the Red Sea, and Mesopotamia, across the Persian Gulf. Contact occurred early on, allowing the Arabs to supplement their seafaring skills with what they learned from the ancient mariners.

Even so, no one knows when these people took to the sea in earnest. Lacking navigable rivers, Arabia's inhabitants did not have access to the riverine trade that allowed the Egyptians and Mesopotamians to learn the art of ships and shipping. Arabia also never produced sufficient wood suitable for building sturdy, seagoing ships, and it lacked iron for nailing them. And yet the Arabs overcame these shortcomings, producing a unique nautical tradition long before it was recorded in writing.

One of the principal characteristics of this tradition was the stitched hull. Because there was no iron for nails, Arab shipbuilders took to sewing the planks of their boats together with fiber. The *Periplus* is the first to mention this practice in its description of the trade with East Africa. Sewn boats also existed along the Red Sea. Describing the Ethiopian coast some one hundred fifty years later, Ptolomy talks about "the man-eating Ethiopians" who lived near the mountains of the moon, and north of them "the Ethiopians who make sewn boats." Along the Persian Gulf coast, stitching was part of local shipbuilding tradition as well, and remained so until well into the twentieth century.

With these sewn craft, Arab seafarers participated in the coastal trade of the Red Sea and the Persian Gulf. When the number of Greek and Roman trading voyages began to grow during the first century B.C., competition increased, but it by no means forced the Arabs out of the shipping business. In fact, the *Periplus* reveals that they continued to ship their goods, from ports like Leuce Come, a trading center along the

Excavations at Sumhuram, not far from Salalah in southern Oman. The Periplus described Sumhuram as one of the safest ports along the South Arabian coast.

The Arabian peninsula had few rivers, none of them navigable. Arabian mariners thus had to learn the art of shipping at sea.

Arabian side of the Red Sea. The nearby coast reportedly had little to recommend it, however. The northern Red Sea was dangerous, the *Periplus* warned, and should be passed "as fast as possible." Further south was the town of Muza, near modern Mokha in Yemen, described as "crowded with Arab shipowners and seafaring men" who "trade with the far-side coast [today's Eritrea, Djibouti, and Somalia] and with Barygaza [Broach]."

Past the Strait of Bāb El-mandeb, the *Periplus* described Ocelis and Arabia Eudaemon (today's Aden), both of which were provisioning ports. Further along the coast was Cane or Qana, where "all the frankincense grown in the country is brought." This port also had "a trade with the far-side market towns [across the Red Sea], and with Barygaza, Scythia [the Indus Valley] and Omana and neighboring Persis." These passages prove that the Arabs were sailing to northern India at least as early as the beginning of the Christian era. The *Periplus* also mentions Arabian shipping in East Africa, noting that Arab ships and traders were found as far south as Rhapta, near the island of Zanzibar.

Arab sailors of that era covered major distances in relatively fragile craft, but until the *Periplus* came along, no one bothered to record the voyages. Unfortunately, the situation did not improve subsequently. There were no Arab historians to record these matters for posterity, and the Greeks' and Romans' lively interest in faraway places soon gave way to different concerns. As a result, nothing comparable to the

ARAB NAVIGATION

As described elsewhere (see pp. 71-73), Arab mariners' dominance on the Indian Ocean was not necessarily due to the quality of their ships, even though the lateen sail represented an important innovation. This form of fore-and-aft rigging made dhows relatively fine monsoon sailors that could progress at a steady pace, but they were uncomfortable ships, seldom decked over except for small platforms fore and aft. Privacy was nonexistent, even for the *nakhoda* or captain, or the owner if he came along. And yet in spite of this, and the very real dangers associated with long voyages, the Arabs managed to control the lucrative sea trade between East and West for more than five hundred years, an achievement that is all too often overlooked. It took hardworking crews and a great deal of navigational skill to accomplish this.

As in other cultures, navigation involved the study of stars, and to that the Arabs were uniquely accustomed. For one thing, finding one's way at sea did not differ a great deal from finding one's way in the desert, which the Arabs had been doing for hundreds of years. For another, the caliber of their scientists was unsurpassed. Muslim astronomers did not necessarily study the night sky with navigational concerns in mind, however; the determination of religious events, which was based in large part on precise astronomical observations, was also of great importance.

From the first caliphates onward, Muslim astronomers began to build on the achievements of the ancients, both in terms of theory and in the manufacturing of precise measuring instruments like the astrolabe. But seafarers used much simpler instruments. They already knew how to deduce latitude from the measurement of the altitude above the horizon of a known star, usually the Pole Star (Polaris) or the sun. When Polaris was too close to the horizon, as it is the nearer one approaches the equator, that information could be obtained from measuring the altitude of another star and tables of declination, included in *rahmani* (see page 73). The science of measuring altitudes was known as *qiyas*.

At sea this was not a science as much as it was an art. Some navigators simply relied on their hands held at arm's length, using their fingers as a unit of measurement. The width of four fingers was considered to measure four *isba'*. Arab mariners accepted that a good day's sail due north would raise the Pole Star one *isba'* from the horizon, a measurement that would figure out at slightly less than one hundred nautical miles, or an average speed of a little over four knots, which seems reasonable. In time the *isba'*, aside from being a measure of altitude, also came to be known as a measure of distance traveled.

For an experienced navigator in known waters, hand measurements might suffice, but further from home in unknown seas that method would have been somewhat risky. For that reason, Arab navigators often used a simple instrument known as a *kamal*. The *kamal* was a small rectangle made out of wood or horn, about two inches by one inch, which had a string inserted at the center. On this string were a number of knots, usually nine, at measured intervals. The end of the string was held in the teeth, the lower edge of the rectangle was placed on the horizon, and the kamal was then moved along the string towards the face until its upper edge was flush with the required star. The knot at which this took place corresponded to a certain altitude, from which a rough measurement of latitude could be derived.

Without an accurate timekeeper, Arab seafarers could not determine their longitude, a shortcoming that was handled by keeping careful watches in the vicinity of landfall. As elsewhere, navigators would have used dead reckoning to estimate where they were and when a coast might be sighted after a long passage at sea. Once they made those calculations, they could refer to the *rahmani* to identify landmarks and thus obtain a precise location.

In China, the Arabs learned of the properties of the lodestone as a means of maintaining direction, a practice they quickly adopted in their own ships. This greatly facilitated maintaining direction at sea; and allowed for more open water sailing on the long voyage to China, with bearings to or from various ports and landmarks quickly incorporated in *rahmani*. The Arabs also had precise nautical charts, which reportedly impressed the first Portuguese explorers to reach the East African seaboard. Unfortunately, none of these appear to have survived the ravages of shipboard life.

It is generally agreed that the zenith of Arab navigation was represented by Shihab al-Din Ahmad Ibn Majid, who is claimed as a native son by both the United Arab Emirates and Oman (he was born circa 1435 in what is now the United Arab Emirates but was then part of Oman). Ibn Majid wrote some forty books on navigational topics, of which *Kitab al-Fawa'id fi usul al-bahr l'qawa'id,* freely translated as the *Book of Profitable Things concerning the Principles and Rules of Navigation*, is unquestionably the most important. Written expressly to consolidate the field, the book is divided into twelve parts, focusing on the science of navigation, seasons, sea routes, natural features, weather conditions, and geography. Only two of the original manuscripts survived.

It is often suggested that it was this Ahmad Ibn Majid who guided Vasco da Gama from Malindi to Calicut, which is possible though not likely. Tradition also states that shortly before his death Ibn Majid lamented the ill effects of the Portuguese arrival in the Indian Ocean, as if he foresaw the dramatic effects this incursion would soon have on Arab seafaring.

Whether or not Ibn Majid handed over the keys to the Indian sea route to Portugal, the seeds to the Arabs' demise had been sown long before. Their lateen sail helped European sailors figure out how to make headway into the wind. Their mathematicians and astronomers perfected the science of navigation, and their sailors and merchants brought China's great nautical inventions—the compass and the rudder—to the West. These contributions proved essential to the development of the West's three-masted ship, and to the science of sending it almost anywhere in the world.

A rare image of a 13th century trading dhow, now kept in the Bibliothèque Nationale in Paris. The ship, her crew and the traders aboard are Persian, not Arab. Depictions of people were seldom made in the Arabian peninsula, explaining why there is hardly any iconography depicting the Golden Age of Arab Seafaring. (Photo: Bibliothèque Nationale)

Periplus or Pliny's *Natural History* was written during the third, fourth, and fifth centuries. For more than two hundred years, the maritime history of the Arabian peninsula remains largely unknown.

Much of the Indian Ocean trade of that period shifted to Persia, where the new Sassanid rulers encouraged sea trade and actively sought to divert the Indian Ocean trade from the Red Sea to the Persian Gulf. They were remarkably successful in their endeavor, reestablishing the Gulf as the principal sea route to the East for the first time in perhaps a thousand years.

Persian merchants began to dominate the trade from East to West, ferrying their goods in large ships from India to the Gulf, and then overland to the Mediterranean. They even ventured as far as China by ship, perhaps as early as the fifth century. But of the ships or their crews we again hardly know anything. Sassanid authors and artists focused mostly on religious matters, seldom on anything as mundane as trade or shipping.

As a result, there are only a few isolated glimpses of Middle Eastern shipping at that time, most of them from the accounts of Chinese merchants who reported seeing Persian ships in the ports of India and Ceylon. Some Chinese traders even went as far as the Persian Gulf, and reported on its maritime doings as well. But their accounts are vague, with most people writing about what they saw or how they felt rather than about the ship and the way it sailed. One traveler, for instance, described the Persian ships arriving from Ceylon and Malaya simply as "big ships." In terms of nautical detail, that obviously is not very useful.

At the same time, these records confirm the Arabs' limited maritime role during this period. Presumably this related to the shifting of Arabia's economic center, from the declining South to northern and central regions. People living in those regions were much more tied to the caravan trade than to the sea, accounting for the Arabs' temporary absence from the seas surrounding the peninsula.

But they would soon be back, and in such a way that the world would never be the same.

EARLY ISLAM

The story of Islam and the subsequent rise of Arab culture and influence begins in this northern region, in and around the city of Mecca. There, in A.D. 610, the Prophet Muhammad began preaching a coherent faith, stressing the omnipotence of Allah as the one and only God, rather than as a member of a diverse pantheon. Muhammad also emphasized the concept of a life after death, an idea new to people who had believed death to be the end of all existence. To these concepts he added a sense of Arabian nationalism, which appealed to a deeply rooted sense of ideals and honor.

Even so, not all Arabs readily accepted the new faith. From its earliest history Islam faced dissent and conflict. Muhammad and his followers turned to violence, ruthlessly suppressing any opposition. Though there were early defeats, they quickly gained ground and Islam expanded accordingly. Even before the Prophet's death in 632, the new faith had been embraced or imposed in much of the Arabian peninsula. Followers of Islam could then afford to be more tolerant, allowing Christians and Jews to practice their own religions, but forcing them and other non-believers to pay a tax.

Muhammad's death threw Islam into momentary confusion. Without a named successor, Muhammad's authority passed to four respected Muslims, chosen as most qualified by their peers. These were the first caliphs, the self-styled Commanders of

the Faithful. Capable men, they patterned themselves after Muhammad, whom they had known personally, and relied on the counsel of trusted friends to make decisions about the course of Islam. Their reigns, however, were often marked by dissent; three of them were murdered by opposing factions.

In spite of these internal conflicts, Islam embarked on a period of conquest to fulfill the wish of the Prophet to carry the Word of God, forcefully if needed, to all corners of the known world. Within ten years of Muhammad's death, Islam shook the foundations of Persia and Byzantium, the two dominant political powers of that time. By the end of the century, it had spread far into Europe, Africa, and Asia. With virtually unparalleled speed, Islam developed from a small religious community to a powerful political empire.

Naturally it was more than religious fervor that propelled this expansion. Drought-stricken Arabia could not produce enough food for its population. Muhammad's desire to export Islam gave the Arabs a reason to invade the fertile regions north and east of them, thereby gaining access to valuable resources. Religion provided the spark for the Arabs' expansion, but the need for resources fanned the flame.

The implications of Islam's growth for world history were vast. By A.D. 650, Muslim armies had conquered Egypt, Syria, Iraq, and most of Persia, providing the Arabs access to the Mediterranean and to the shores of the Persian Gulf. During the reign of

the Umayyad Caliphate (661 - 749), the empire expanded to the borders of India and China in the east, and to North Africa and Spain in the west. In the process the Arabs not only created the dominant political power of that era but also, by controlling the trade routes between East and West, were on the verge of becoming a major economic force.

Nonetheless, to realize this potential, the Arabs had to go to sea. Though reluctant to do so, northern Arabs realized they needed a naval presence to counter the Byzantine Empire and its well-organized navy. As they expanded along the eastern Mediterranean seaboard and into Egypt, they gained the means to do so. Here there was an established maritime tradition, enabling the Arabs to build a respectable navy and obtain the necessary crews and bases. With these, they faced the Byzantine fleet in A.D. 655 off the southern Turkish coast at Dhat al-Sawari, in the so-called Battle of the Masts. Though heavily outnumbered, the Arab fleet managed to convert the confrontation into a battle across decks that suited its fighters, and to resoundingly defeat the opposing fleet.

The port of Ayega near Sur, in the Persian Gulf. Islam would have a profound effect on the relationship between the Arabs and the sea, because ships were needed to carry the Word of God to all corners of the world. These ships, in turn, enabled the Arabs to control the trade between East and West.

Although the victory seemed to open the way to Constantinople and the establishment of the Arabs as the heirs to Byzantium's maritime legacy, events transpired otherwise. In spite of several attempts, the Arabs failed to subdue the city and, though they proved courageous fighters at sea, their navy never dominated the Mediterranean the way the Romans and others had before. For that, the fleet simply was not sufficiently organized, nor was it commanded by experienced seamen. Arab chronicles speak of entire fleets vanishing in the Mediterranean's dreaded autumn storms, losses that contributed to a deeply rooted fear of the sea. "Trust it little, fear it much" wrote one Arab scholar in response to a question by one of the first caliphs. "Man at sea is an insect on a splinter, now engulfed, then scared to death."

TRADE ROUTES

This apprehension notwithstanding, Arab mariners excelled at more individualistic maritime endeavors like trading and raiding. Operating from North African bases, Arab pirates made much of the Mediterranean unsafe for Western shipping. To the east the Byzantine navy was able to keep these activities under control, but for several centuries the western Mediterranean remained unsafe, greatly hindering the development of trade.

The Indian Ocean, in contrast, was a region of peace. And it was here that the Arabs set their mark on the world's maritime history by sailing regularly not only to India and Ceylon, but beyond as far as China and Korea. Beginning in the eighth century, this trade route was by far the longest sea route in regular use, and it would remain so until Spain and Portugal set out on the world's oceans 750 years later.

There is little doubt that efficient and well-organized governments at either end of the route had something to do with this flourishing trade. From the early seventh century, China was ruled by the Tang dynasty (618 - 907), which brought the country a period of prolonged peace and great cultural and economic growth. At the route's other end, the Umayyad (661 - 749) and Abbasid (750 - 870) caliphates reigned over the world of Islam at its peak.

Unlike their predecessors, China's Tang emperors welcomed foreign trade and contacts. Since they had no maritime ambitions of their own, most of the trade to and from the West was carried initially by Indian and Persian ships, and from the middle of the eighth century by the Arabs, or *Ta-shih*, as the Chinese knew them.

At first they made only a few voyages, but from the ninth century onward the Arabs began to sail to China regularly. With this increased frequency came more information about the trade, not only from the Chinese but from Arab traders and sailors as well. Many of their accounts are stories of tempest-tossed seas and untold dangers that no doubt became exaggerated over the years. But woven throughout is a good deal of information on nautical and geographical matters, providing a unique glimpse into the world of Arab shipping.

The story of Sulayman the Merchant provides an excellent example. Compiled in 851 by an unknown writer, it describes a trading voyage from Siraf in the Persian Gulf to Canton, today's Guangzhou. We do not know whether Sulayman the Merchant existed, but it does not really matter. His story is probably a compilation of reports from various travelers, in much the same way that a romanticized version of later voyages developed into the well-known tales of Sinbad the Sailor. And like his fictional colleague, Sulayman left us a vivid description of the voyage, with information on life in India and China thrown in for good measure.

Siraf, which was located on the Iranian Persian Gulf coast south of Shiraz, owed its existence to the trade with India. Built along a barren coast, it had few resources other than its harbor, and during the eighth century it became one of the western gateway ports of the China trade. Another terminal was located in Al-Basrah at the mouth of the Persian Gulf, but navigating the headwaters of the Gulf was difficult, and eventually much of its trade shifted further south. From Al-Basrah cargoes of linen, wool, and cotton, as well as iron ore and precious metals, were ferried in smaller boats to Siraf, to be transferred onto the large China traders. Many ships also left from ports like Muscat and Sohar further south along the Omani coast.

Vessels sailing from Siraf would try to reach the southern Gulf by late November, in order to take advantage of the northeast monsoon on their crossing to the Indian Malabar coast. After stocking up in Quilon, Kulam Mali, or another Malabar port, the ships continued across the Bay of Bengal to Kaleh Bar in the Malay Peninsula. From there they sailed through the Straits of Malacca, and then turned north along the coast of Indochina to Sandar Fulat (also known as Sanf Fulaw), an island off the Vietnamese coast, then known as the Gate to China. Finally, the vessels crossed the South China Sea to Hainan and followed the Chinese coast to Canton, or Khanfu as the Arabs called it. Some ships continued on to Hangzhou and Korea, and a few may even have made it as far as Japan.

Each of the legs to Khanfu took about a month but, along with time spent provisioning, the outward voyage could take as long as six months. Most of the summer and early fall was spent doing business, trading goods brought from the Persian Gulf

A detail from a tomb in the Arab graveyard in Quanzhou, China. Arab traders settled in this part of China as early as the eighth century.

The Indian Malabar coast also experienced strong Arab influence, with large trading dhows regularly visiting its ports.

for spices, silks, ceramics, and aromatics like camphor and musk. By fall, the ships were ready for the return voyage.

Taking advantage of the northeast monsoon, the vessels followed the same route to Kaleh Bar in Malaya. From there they went across the Bay of Bengal to India, reaching the Malabar Coast early in the year. With the northeast monsoon still blowing it was impossible to head directly to the Persian Gulf, so instead they set a course to Shihr or Raysut on the South Arabian coast. The first breezes of the southwest monsoon in April then allowed the ships to head northeast along the coast of Oman and into the Persian Gulf toward their home ports. In all, most of these voyages took about eighteen months, giving the owners and crews about six months to sell the cargo, buy new goods, and prepare the vessels for another trip.

There was trade from the Red Sea to India and China as well, which had its main terminal at Aden. Some ships left from Jiddah, but little is known about these voyages prior to the tenth century, when Egypt began to replace the Persian Gulf region as Islam's center of population and wealth. But by that time, the frequency of the China voyages had begun to decline. Both the Tang and Abbasid empires began crumbling during the late ninth century, and trade between the two inevitably suffered.

Commerce with East Africa was also flourishing. Although there is little information about this region since its last mention in the *Periplus*, it appears that trading had continued all along, albeit on a smaller scale. In all likelihood the Sassanid Persians con-

trolled the trade in the centuries prior to Islam, but after the Revelation the Arabs returned and reclaimed the North-South routes they had once initiated.

Little had changed in the intervening years. The products first obtained from Africa—ivory, tortoise shells, ambergris and rhinoceros horns—were still in demand, and throughout the centuries vast amounts were shipped from East Africa to Arabian and Indian ports. Many exotic products went to China and the East. Ivory, in particular, was much sought after in China and India, where it was carved into luxury items like palanquins or chess and backgammon pieces. Ambergris, an opaque secretion of the sperm whale intestine, also went mostly to China, where it was used to preserve the scent of perfumes.

As on their voyages to India and beyond, Arab sailors took advantage of the monsoonal changes to reach their destinations. A trip from Oman to East Africa, for instance, could be made in less than three weeks during February and March when the northeast winds blew and the North Equatorial Current was strongest. The return trip took advantage of the southwest monsoon in April.

During the tenth and eleventh centuries East Africa became a prosperous region, with towns like Kilwa, Zanzibar, Mombasa, Kilifu, Pemba, Malindi, Lamu, Pate, and Sofala benefiting from a vibrant trade. Arab traders had founded or expanded many of these places, but they retained a colorful indigenous character, creating a unique Swahili culture. Ruled as independent city-states by Arab sheiks, they were self-sufficient, producing their own food and plenty of products for trading. They grew rich but somewhat complacent. And that would prove a costly misjudgment in the years to come.

Many Swahili towns lost their wealth and power. Of once mighty Pate in northern Kenya, only some ruins are left.

TECHNOLOGY

The Arabs maintained this expansive trading network with what were, by all accounts, relatively fragile ships. Few, if any, pictures exist to show us what they looked like, but various literary sources indicate that the ships had changed relatively little since the Arabs' first forays into the Indian Ocean one thousand years earlier.

The hulls of Arabian dhows of the tenth century derived directly from the vessels that sailed the waters of the Red Sea and Persian Gulf from about 1000 B.C. They were double-ended, coming to a point at stem and stern, and carried a side rudder on the quarter. The planks were sewn rather than nailed together, as the *Periplus* had observed at the beginning of the Christian era. This limited the maximum size of the ships, accounting for the relative continuity in hull shape.

Some Arab writers maintained that a sewn hull was more pliant and could be expected to withstand a harsh landing on a sandy beach or even grounding on a coral reef. But aside from that, it made for a poor ship. A sewn hull was weak, leaky, and quite unsafe. If just one of the bindings broke at sea, the crew could face a major problem. And yet, the Arabs stubbornly stuck to their fibers, even after they could import iron to make nails from other parts of the Islam Empire. Perhaps economics played a role, since coconut fiber was much cheaper than iron nails imported from India or the West; more importantly, Arab seamen were notoriously conservative. Some were convinced of the existence of magnetic rocks in the Red Sea and Indian Ocean that could

pull iron-nailed ships apart. Others believed that iron corroded much faster in the Indian Ocean than elsewhere, causing nailed craft to literally fall apart on long voyages.

Whatever the explanation, these beliefs made Arab seamen put up with uncomfortable and dangerous voyages. Shipwreck by storm was a common phenomenon, as most contemporary accounts make clear, and those who were spared faced long months at sea in overcrowded conditions, exposed to the elements, continuously bailing out the bilge, and always on guard for uncharted reefs, storms, pirates, and a host of other perils. It is a tribute to the Arabs' courage and skill that a sufficient number of ships not only reached China, but also returned, their holds filled with riches from Cathay.

Arab accounts voiced few complaints about these shortcomings, perhaps because their authors were unaware of alternatives or simply accepted whatever fate lay ahead. But those who could compare these ships to vessels elsewhere were unimpressed. European travelers, in particular, were appalled. "These ships are mighty frail and uncouth with no iron in them," wrote John of Montecorvino, "and so if the twine breaks there is a breach indeed!" "The men always, or nearly always, must stand in a pool to bail out the water," added Jordanus. And Marco Polo was even more critical: "These ships are wretched affairs and many of them get lost for they have no iron fastenings and are only stitched together with twine made from the husk of the Indian

Wooden dhows remain in demand, with fishermen in the Red Sea and Persian Gulf still ordering large numbers of them, albeit without sail and rigging. Along the less affluent East African coast, the mast and lateen sail remain very much in use (right).

nut. ... Hence 't is a perilous business to make a voyage in one of these ships and many of them are lost in that Sea of India; the storms are often terrible."

As unimpressed as these observers may have been, their accounts were written several hundred years after the Arabs' first China voyages, at a time when Western countries had not even begun to develop a long-distance maritime tradition of their own. Moreover, few of these travelers had a nautical background. When Portuguese navigator Pedro Álvares Cabral first saw sewn Gujarati ships in Malindi in the early sixteenth century, he called them "very well built, of good timber, and stitched with cords for they have no nails."

Early European accounts also failed to recognize the Arabs' contribution to maritime technology. Arabian hulls may have been creaky and leaky, but above deck, in the rigging, their builders had made very important improvements. Whereas European vessels of the tenth century were rigged with a single square sail, Arab dhows used a fore-and-aft lateen-like sail, from which the forward corner had been cut. The West's rigging was fine for large, bulky ships and provided a measure of stability in heavy seas, but it was difficult to handle in restricted waters and almost useless for sailing into the wind. The Arabs' lateen or settee sail, in contrast, was much better suited for narrow-water sailing and could keep much closer to the wind. In fact, it was one of the first sails that enabled ships to actually make headway into the wind.

Though triangular sails were also used in the Pacific, the typical lateen is generally believed to be an Arab invention. Unfortunately, there is nothing in Arab art or literature to confirm this. No pictures of Arab ships exist prior to the thirteenth century, largely because Islam did not encourage that type of art. Limited information on the Arabs' rigging configuration can be gleaned from literary sources, but it is not

much. Marco Polo, for instance, observed only one mast, though Arab authors often speak of two. The sails were woven from palm fronds in some regions and from sailcloth in others. Most vessels probably set only one large sail on each mast, though they carried smaller ones to use during foul weather.

A similar form of sail was used in the Pacific, as Europeans seafarers discovered when they reached this area in the sixteenth century. Although this Pacific form probably developed independently from the practice in the Near East, this does not detract from the Arabs' contribution to maritime technology because they introduced the practice to the Mediterranean and the West. Without that contribution, European mariners would have remained confined to coastal waters much longer.

Arab mariners also developed sophisticated navigational techniques and detailed *rahmani* or rutters—books that contained information on the exact latitudes of ports, headlands, and other markers, as well as reefs, winds, sailing directions, currents, depths, and whatever else a captain or pilot would want to know. *Rahmani* were usually compiled by navigators themselves, for they knew best what information was essential, but they also drew from data compiled by professional travelers and geographers.

The dean of the Arabian geographers was Ibn Khurdadbih of Baghdad, whose *Book of Kingdoms and Routes* (A.D. 846) described the land and sea routes to India and China. Other famous travelers included Ibn Fadlan, who traveled throughout Russia,

DHOWS

The origin of the word *dhow* is unclear. In East Africa certain sailing vessels were called *daus*, and it is possible that the generic Western term for the ships of Arabian and Indian waters may have derived from that. After all, the Portuguese—the first Europeans to reach the area by sea—came up along the East African coast, where they would undoubtedly have heard the word, interested as they were in all things nautical. That way the term would have entered Western lexicons via a Portuguese detour. Others assume the term derives from an obscure Persian vessel called *dawh*, but that is not certain either. Until recently most Arabs or Persians, when asked, would not even have know what a dhow was. They referred to their ships by specific names, some of which are described below. The term does not exist in the Arab language, though most Arabs recognize it now from English usage.

Whatever its precise path, Western languages define the term as a group of ships used in East African, Arab, and Indian waters, whose main characteristic is the large lateen sail. Actually that is not entirely correct because most Arab and Indian vessels used what is know as a settee sail—a lateen from which the foremost corner had been shortened to create a short

luff or leading edge. But today that distinction is no longer important. After all, sailing dhows are rapidly disappearing, especially in and around the Arabian peninsula. What matters now is survival, not the specifics of the sail.

Though sailing dhows are becoming a rare sight in their place of origin, the typical dhow-shaped hull will survive for some time to come. There are still plenty of dhows being built around the Indian Ocean littoral, albeit without a mast and rigging. Especially in the Persian Gulf states, where fuel is very inexpensive, a diesel engine is now the preferred form of propulsion. But even here fishermen and local traders cling to the shapes of old, ordering a sufficient number of wooden vessels to keep dhow builders in business, at least for some time to come.

Although dhows are not simple ships, their construction has always been a relatively uncomplicated affair, at least to the Western eye. For one thing, there never were plans or blueprints. The ship was built by eye and experience, and it still is in dhow construction yards, meaning that it is hard if not impossible to find two dhows that are exactly alike.

Prior to the Europeans' arrival, shipbuilders usually laid a keel on the ground and then fastened horizontal planks to it on each side and to each other edge to edge (or carvel-like) by stitches of coir. Teak was the wood of choice, though it had to be imported from India; no suitable shipbuilding wood grows in the Arabian peninsula. The trade in wood, as a consequence, is very old. It was already well established when the *Periplus of the Erythraean Sea* was written, and probably long before that.

Early sources do not mention the use of any form of internal framework such as ribs, though larger vessels would have required them. But ribs were always fitted after the planks were in place—an ancient form of shipbuilding known as shell construction. This made sense when the planks were stitched together because each plank was attached to the one below. Interestingly, the practice has survived the switch to nailed construction, though it certainly does not make the process any easier.

But dhow yards are not necessarily run according to what is easiest. Although power tools are readily available in every dhow yard, the old tools are never far out of reach. In fact, even today a complement of tools is used that can be seen on the walls of four-thousand-year-old Egyptian tombs: hammers, bow-drills, and especially adzes. A master-builder or *ustadh,* whose authority is based on many years of experience, usually supervises the work. Under him are the *najjars* or carpenters, and *muhandis*—a term that can be roughly translated as engineers.

Once the hull is nearing completion, caulking begins, using a mixture of fiber or raw cotton impregnated with fish or coconut oil. Below the waterline the hull is covered with *chunam:* a protective coating made by boiling oil, animal fat, or resin with lime. Above the waterline several coatings of fish or vegetable oil are applied to give the teak its warm and rich appearance.

Today's dhows are a relatively generic type of vessel that has been created to accommodate engines and improve ease of handling. Their predecessors came in many shapes and forms, some of which survived well into the twentieth century, but not quite into the current one. As a result no classification can ever be complete or even accurate, given the many names for similar types of vessels. Among the most important types of dhows and coastal craft were (and are) the following:

Boom

Also known as a *bum, bhum,* or *boum,* the *boom* was a trading dhow in widespread use all along the Arabian peninsula and as far as the Indian coast. The sailing boom, which worked until well into the twentieth century, plied the Indian Ocean for well over a thousand years with relatively few changes. Like other dhow types, booms were modified somewhat to compete with European vessels, but the vessel remained double-ended. It was relatively easy to recognize with its high, straight stem-post, set at forty-five degrees, which was built out into a kind of planked (non-functional) bowsprit, often decorated with a simple design in black-and-white. On many booms a vertically stepped mizzenmast supplemented the forward-raking mainmast.

A dhow approaches the island of Mozambique. The design of the vessels was influenced by the Portuguese, who ruled the island for more than 450 years.

The shape of the shu'ai, with its projecting strakes, survives in many fishing dhows along the Persian Gulf.

Baggala

Also know as the *baghlah* or *baghla,* the *baggala* was one of the largest trading dhows operating in the East-West trades. It was characterized by its arched transom stern, pierced by five window apertures and often elaborately carved. The square stern and high poop were a direct result of European influence, with local builders incorporating the design in order to create more competitive and impressive-looking vessels. With lengths up to forty meters (135 feet), *baggalas* often stepped up to three masts, and reached sizes of up to 500 tons.

Sambuk

Derived from the Portuguese word *sambuco,* the *sambuk* was one of the most common dhows around the Arabian peninsula. Its main characteristics were its stem, curved above the waterline, and its high quarterdeck with railings along its sides, ending in a square (or transom) stern from which strakes projected on both sides. Being true all-purpose working ships, *sambuks* do not sport the elaborate carving of the baggala, but some of them are more lavishly painted than any other dhow. Especially along the western coasts of the Arabian peninsula, this results in some very colorful ships.

Shu'ai

There are many spellings for this vessel type, from *say* to *saiyah, shewee* to *shuei.* Smaller than a *sambuk,* the *shu'ai* is otherwise quite similar, with the exception of the stem—curved for the *sambuk* and nearly always straight on the *shu'ai.* Like the *sambuk,* the *shu'ai* sports a low bow, a delicate sheer, and an upswept quarterdeck (or poop) with railing. And like their larger cousins, *shu'ais* have a square stern with projecting strakes. The sailing variants usually had a single mast. The hull design still survives in many wooden fishing dhows built along the Persian Gulf.

Ganjah

Also known as a *ganja, gancha* or *khansha,* this was a large sailing dhow, characterized by a distinctive figurehead, usually the stylized head of a bird looking backwards (which is of Indian origin). There was a transom stern aft, shaped like a heraldic shield—a seventeenth-century remnant that remained in use until well into the twentieth century. Some *ganjahs* included carved quarter galleries in the stern, which were copied from Western ships. On Arab ships, however, they were never more than a decorative element, for the space behind usually served as storage space rather than living quarters. A superb example of a mid-twentieth-century *ganjah* is preserved at Sur in Oman, one of the principal shipbuilding ports along the Persian Gulf.

Zarook

Like the boom, the *zarook* is an ancient design, double-ended and with masts heavily raked forward. Originally developed in the Red Sea, it is still built along its shores, though mostly without elaborate rigging. But since fuel prices in countries like Yemen are considerably higher than along the Persian Gulf, many traditional dhows still step a smaller mast, to take advantage of favorable winds.

Jaliboot

The *jaliboot* (*jalbut* or *jalbaut*) is a small- to medium-sized dhow from the head of the Persian Gulf. Though its rigging is similar to that of a small *sambuk* or *shu'ai*, the ship is distinguished by its straight vertical stem, which was quite uncommon for Arab ships and hence probably the result of European influence.

Bedan

The *bedan* or *bedeni* was a dhow from the southern Persian Gulf, with a false clipper-like stem and tall pointed stern—a profile that made it easy to recognize. Similar ships with a very raked stem were known as *baqaras*. None of these ships survive commercially.

Jahazi

A small East African dhow, still quite frequently seen from Mozambique to northern Kenya. The ship has a vertical stem and square stern.

Kotia

One of several types of Indian deep-sea dhows, also known as *kutiyah* or *kothia*. The ship had a curved stem with bird motif facing aft. Like other Indian dhows, the arched transom was often beautifully carved. A few of these ships still operate commercially, though their days appear to be numbered. The same is true for the *thoni* or *dhoni*, a sailing dhow from southern India and Sri Lanka that is one of the largest sailing dhows still carrying cargoes.

An Indian dhow unloads its cargo in the old port of Mombasa, Kenya. A few large dhows still cross the Indian Ocean, but they are the last survivors of a dying breed.

and Al Mas'udi, who covered the known world during the tenth century, penning down his findings in *Meadows of Gold and Mines of Precious Stones*. His book does not say much about meadows of gold but a fancy title, then as now, possibly helped increase readership.

Also consulted were Ibn Haukal, whose *Of Ways and Provinces* described three decades of travel throughout the Muslim world; and Al Idrisi, who traveled throughout Europe and Central Asia and is best known for a world map he produced for Norman ruler Roger II in Sicily. But the most indefatigable traveler of all was Ibn Battuta, who set out from Tangier for a pilgrimage to Mecca in 1326 and did not return until twenty-five years and some seventy-five thousand miles later. Compiling and transcribing his reports, it was said, took more than thirty years.

This interaction among astronomers, mathematicians, navigators, and geographers enabled the Arabs to compile superb nautical directions. Some, like the work of the Omani navigator Ahmad Ibn Majid, who wrote at the end of the fifteenth century, reached a state of near-perfection. His work included extremely detailed sailing directions, along with astronomical observations and instructions for calculating a position at sea, including a sophisticated attempt to determine longitude by means of lunar distances. Ibn Majid is also credited with improving the magnetic compass for use at sea. In a very real sense, he embodied Arabian nautical know-how at its pinnacle.

THE DECLINE

It is popularly believed that it was Ibn Majid who guided Vasco da Gama and his fleet from the Kenyan port of Malindi to Calicut in 1498, opening the Indian Ocean and the riches of the East to Portugal and the West. Since it would have been a considerable coincidence if two of that era's most capable navigators were in the same spot at the same time, this is doubtful, though it would not have been all that much of an irony. By that time all of the Arabs' great nautical contributions—the lateen sail, the astrolabe, and the more refined quadrant, trigonometry, logarithms, and astronomical tables—had already found their way into Europe. All of them helped the West break out onto the oceans. Whether it was Ibn Majid or someone else who guided the Portuguese to India, it was only the final act in a process that was irreversible. By then the Arabs had already sown the seeds of their own maritime demise.

Vasco da Gama's arrival in India shattered the relatively peaceful political and economic system of the western Indian Ocean. For the independent city-states along the East African seaboard, it was a disaster. Prizing their independence, they had never bothered to organize anything resembling even a loose political confederation, making them vulnerable to outsiders. Realizing this, the Portuguese took advantage of it. Though they encountered a level of civilization far more advanced than expected, they ruthlessly attacked each port, with the exception of Malindi. By 1512, only fourteen years after their arrival in the Indian Ocean, the Portuguese had taken control of the entire East African littoral, as well as Hormuz in the Persian Gulf and large parts of western India.

For Arab shipping the results were disastrous. After having dominated the Indian Ocean for hundreds of years, Arab ships were relegated to bulk and local trades. The Red Sea and Persian Gulf, which had been the major sea routes from East to West since the beginning of recorded time, lost their importance. From this point forward, the East's most valuable goods were carried directly to Europe around the Cape of Good Hope. The Arabs lost their role as exclusive middlemen and with it their customary sources of wealth and power.

Arab ships changed in response to the emergence of European vessels. The traditional double-ended vessels began to support a square transom stern and a high poop deck, mimicking the design of Western ships. Soon shipbuilders also began to nail their vessels, in a desperate attempt to imitate the Portuguese enemy. This enabled them to build larger dhows, but had no effect on their participation in the trade from East to West.

The Portuguese had nothing less than a monopoly in mind, exerting absolute control not only over the principal commodities but also over their carriage. They discouraged Arab trade by requiring that dhows have Portuguese permits. For the first time ever, Arab cargoes were taxed, changing the free trade system that had existed in the Indian Ocean since time immemorial. Inevitably Arab and local shipping declined, particularly in East Africa but also in the Persian Gulf and along the Indian coast.

Many dhow crews did not abide by the European rules, and continued to do business as they had before. If caught they risked their ships and cargoes, and often their lives. Unable to control all trades and cargoes, the Portuguese thus helped to bring about a new role for dhows: the large-scale smuggling of contraband. Though a far cry from their proud role during the Golden Age of Arab shipping, smuggling suited Arabian vessels, which were much faster than the vessels that were supposed to control them.

When Portugal's control and influence in the region diminished during the seventeenth century, the Arab crews found that the danger of being caught decreased, though it was only a matter of time before others began patrolling the Indian Ocean. During the nineteenth century, for instance, British frigates were sent to the region to eradicate Arab smugglers and slavers. British reports made clear that it was hard to keep up with a well-manned dhow. It was not until after the 1850s, when the Royal Navy turned to auxiliary steam engines, that it began to make some headway. Even then the fastest dhows often got away, for coal was expensive and it took hours to raise steam and give chase.

Smuggling is still widespread throughout the Indian Ocean; only the cargoes have changed. With the decline of the slave trade, dhows began to carry illegal immigrants from poverty-stricken areas in India, Pakistan, and Iran to the wealthy oil sheikdoms of the Persian Gulf, and they still do. During the political upheavals in East Africa in the 1960s, dhows also brought people to more stable areas. They have been heavily involved in the smuggling of ivory to the Persian Gulf, and they continue to carry gold, drugs, liquor, and other contraband.

Although these are questionable trades, there is little doubt that without smuggling there would be even fewer dhows still at work. Moreover, not all the contraband is as harmful. Sometimes it just involves the carriage of manufactured goods like radios and refrigerators, to evade the high taxes assessed on them. And many dhows never smuggle anything at all. Especially along the East African and Indian coasts, dhows are involved in perfectly legal activities, carrying commodities ranging from mangrove poles to perishables and dried fish from port to port along the coast, as they have done for thousands of years.

Even in the face of the vast industrial and social changes that have taken place in Arab countries, dhows have managed to retain a role, largely as a result of their enormous versatility. Steamships need ports and docking facilities. Dhows, in contrast, can enter and service places that do not have any of these. Modern ships also need a sufficient amount of cargo to make a trip profitable. Dhows, on the other hand, are available to carry smaller amounts at any time. They are slower and may have to wait for a spell of bad weather to pass, but fortunately speed and efficiency do not rule everything everywhere.

Perhaps this slower pace, more than anything else, explains the continued existence of the dhow. When the Europeans arrived in the Indian Ocean five hundred years ago, things changed dramatically, but not in the ways of local ships. Though they were excluded from the main trades between East and West, they continued going about their business. After all, these ships had sailed these waters for more than a thousand years, and they had done well. No doubt many thought they would weather the arrival of the Europeans as well, and survive another thousand years.

They now have survived for half of that period. Whether they will survive the second half is doubtful, but hopefully they will not be forgotten. For these ships and their sailors played an instrumental role in one of the great chapters in the story of people and the sea.

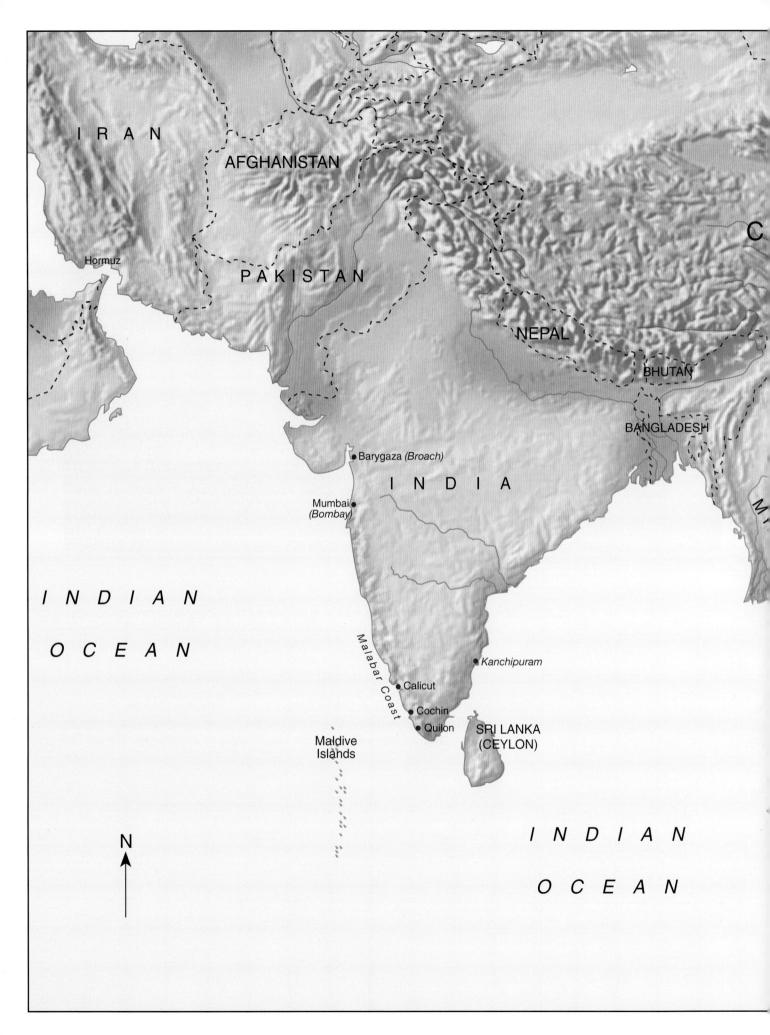

THE DRAGON AT SEA

'In the fifth year of the reign of Xuande Emperor, in the intercalary

twelfth moon, on the sixth day the ships started from Dragon Bay.

On the tenth day, they came to Deer Island. On the twentieth day

they passed through the channel and the next day they reached

Liu chia chiang. In the sixth year, in the second moon, on the twenty

sixth day they arrived at the Min River. In the twelfth moon,

on the ninth day they left the river and traveled for sixteen days.

On the twenty fourth day they arrived at Chan city. In the seventh

year, in the first moon, on the eleventh day the ships left.

They traveled for twenty five days.'

Thus begins the account by Zhu Yunming of one of the greatest sea voyages of all time, led by one of the greatest explorers of all time. Chances are many will not recognize the name of this explorer: Zheng He, commander of the Chinese Ming fleet on its seven voyages to the "Western Seas."

The last of these voyages, this one consisted of more than a hundred ships, given such names as *Pure Harmony, Lasting Tranquility* and *Peaceful Crossing*. Aboard were 27,550 men, among them, according to Zhu, officers, banner troops, fire leaders, helmsmen, anchormen, interpreters, accountants, doctors, iron-anchor mechanics, caulkers, scaffold builders, sailors, boatmen, and many others.

Zhu Yunming's account monotonously lists their ports of call: Man-la-chia, Hsi-lan shan, the country of Kuli, and Lu-I-hu-mo-ssu, names in which, with a bit of imagination, one can recognize Malacca, Ceylon, Calicut, and Hormuz. Some vessels sailed even further, to Aden and Mecca in the Red Sea, the Maldive Islands, and Mogadishu along the East African coast. The fleet did not return to its home port of Nanjing until "the eighth year, in the sixth moon on the twenty first day," or July 7, 1433. It had been gone for two-and-a-half years.

At the same time, along the northwest coast of Africa, a small, single-masted ship was cautiously inching its way south. Commanded by Gil Eanes, it had been sent by Portugal's Henry the Navigator to round Cape Bojador. Though their destination was only a minor cape along the African coast, the ship's occupants were terrified. They were convinced the world ended at Bojador and that, if they sailed beyond, they

would disappear forever. As they neared the cape, they refused to go on, forcing Eanes to turn back and set a course for Lagos, their home port.

One year later, Eanes succeeded in sailing beyond the feared cape, passing the boundary where knowledge ended and myth took over. In a very real sense he opened the way for later explorers, but the contrast with China's show of maritime prowess on the eastern side of the continent could not have been greater. His was one small vessel with an unruly, terrified crew, who had no idea where they were heading. Zheng He, in contrast, commanded a fleet of more than a hundred vessels, some of them reportedly measuring three thousand tons, manned by thousands of well-organized and disciplined men. This fleet knew exactly where it was heading because it had been there several times before.

Yet it was the Portuguese who would eventually rule the seas and who, barely one hundred years later, would contest China's hegemony in its very own waters. Zheng He's last voyage marked the end of China's maritime ambitions, while Eanes's comparatively pitiful effort along the North African coast heralded the ascendancy of a new oceanic order.

To understand what happened we must not only study what drove the Portuguese and the West in general across the oceans, but also what transpired in the East. What happened to China's powerful fleets? Why did China turn its back on the sea at a time when it could have ruled the oceans and the trade that was carried across them?

The ancient Chinese learned the art of ships and shipping on the country's many rivers. According to Chinese mythology, these first navigational efforts benefited from considerable divine assistance.

There are no simple answers, for China's relationship with the sea has always been a complicated, almost ambiguous affair. The story is further complicated by a lack of visual clues and trustworthy literary references. Even so, it is clear that China at certain times in its long history exhibited great maritime ambitions, and that the keys to the West's eventual supremacy over the seas are to be found in the Far East as much as in Europe.

CHINESE ORIGINS

Unlike most areas, China has some writings on the origin of its ships. Unfortunately, they are mythical accounts, referring to what happened during the country's nebulous Legendary Period, long before recorded history. According to one of these, the *I Ching* or *Book of Changes*, Fu Hsi, the first of the Five Great Rulers of this Legendary Period, invented the boat. As one of the book's appendices explains, Fu Hsi taught his people to fish and to build boats by "hewing planks and shaping and planing wood."

Fu Hsi lists more than impressive maritime credentials. He is also credited with the development of the *pa-kua*, the eight mystic diagrams that play an important role in Chinese divination, brought to him by a "dragon horse" from heaven, or so it was said. When Fu Hsi's earthly rule came to an end, he appropriately retired by ascending to heaven on a dragon's back, but not before instructing his subjects on how to build carts as well.

Subsequent legendary rulers are also accorded maritime fame. A later account claims that boats were not introduced until Huang Di, third Legendary Emperor,

needed them to defeat his enemies. Perhaps this account referred to ships used for warfare, rather than for commerce. Huang Di is also said to have introduced the oar and the compass, though he is remembered principally as the inventor of writing and weapons.

Finally, the great Emperor Yu, fifth Legendary Ruler and "tamer of floods," deserves nautical honors as well. Though Yu reportedly had "a tiger's nose, a large mouth, and ears with three openings," he went on to become China's most celebrated hydrological engineer, masterminding the draining of immense swamps and improving the navigability of rivers. Naturally, this greatly aided the development of early agriculture and transport in the country.

Traditional Chinese history implies that all great inventions, including the boat, stem from this Legendary Period, but there are doubts about this. For one thing, Fu Hsi and his successors are thought to have lived from around 2850 to 2200 B.C. Although we know little about the people who lived in China at that time, they probably developed rafts or floating objects of one kind or another well before then. Their land, with its two great riverine systems—the Huang He (Yellow River) and the Yangtze—would have invited some form of nautical development at an early stage.

The *Huainanzi,* a book dating back to 122 B.C., suggests that leaves drifting on a stream led to the development of rafts. It also suggests that "he who looked on a

The Chinese learned much from nature. Leaves floating on a pond provided the inspiration for rafts, it was said. The shape of these first rafts can still be recognized in small craft today (below).

hollow log floating on the water was the first shipbuilder," which is probably closer to the truth. The early Chinese did not have to wait until Fu Hsi and his successors descended from heaven to make that connection. But if these stories tell us anything, it is that boats and water transport were important in early China. Otherwise, they would not have been mentioned so prominently in the accounts of the Middle Kingdom's distant past.

Other than these references, there is little or no information about China's earliest vessels. None of them survive, and detailed visual representations did not appear until much later, making it difficult to state with certainty how China's earliest craft developed. Some probably derived from floating logs and dugouts, as in other parts of the world, or from different materials, like skins stretched over a wooden frame. Bamboo's availability in the southern and central parts of the country makes it likely that the first craft there were mostly bamboo rafts. And it is generally believed that the Chinese developed some of their later vessels directly from these rafts.

The earliest Chinese depiction of a boat, or rather a pictograph that represented the concept of a ship or boat, was found on a set of bones accidentally dug up by farmers in the late nineteenth century. Archaeologists figured out that the bones, which were probably used to try to determine what the gods had in store, dated back to the seventeenth century B.C. They also discovered that the symbols were more than simple pictographs. The markings possessed a logic that revealed them to be China's earliest form of writing. Virtually overnight they pushed back written records of the Middle Kingdom's history by nearly a thousand years, to the Shang dynasty of the second millennium B.C.

The pictographs on the so-called Oracle Bones opened a window on a fascinating Bronze-Age culture. The Shang Chinese used bamboo for writing and books, and cowrie shells as a monetary unit. They also had a well-developed system of water-borne commerce. Aside from the boat pictograph, there were characters for "receiving from hand to hand" (or trading), propelling a boat, and even caulking the seams of a boat. These imply that nautical technology had developed well beyond the bamboo raft.

During the subsequent Zhou dynasty (c. 1030 - 221 B.C.), China underwent a period of advanced intellectual and technological development. Scholars and philosophers roamed the country, among them Confucius (551 - 479 B.C.), whose vision of a united and stable China, ruled by moral suasion and ritual, would profoundly affect the country's political system. But Confucianism did not prevail until long after Confucius's death. His China remained a divided country, where many states were constantly at war with one another.

Nonetheless, a money-based economy gradually replaced the country's feudal system, agricultural production methods were improved, and massive water projects were initiated. Unfortunately, we know little of the ships and shipping of that time. To get a first glimpse of China's maritime activities, we have to wait until the Qin dynasty unified the country in 222 B.C.

THE QIN AND HAN DYNASTIES

China's unification under Emperor Qin Shihuangdi is traditionally seen as the birth of orderly civilization in the Middle Kingdom. Though its reign was short, the Qin dynasty installed a bureaucracy that subsequent dynasties would largely adopt. It divided the country into a number of provinces, each with its own regional government; standardized the language; established a network of roads; and made uniform measures such as weights and lengths, and even the gauge of carts and chariots.

During Qin times China also began to build its Great Wall to protect the country from the barbarian tribes to the north. But the Qin emperor was not interested only in retaining his territory; he also wanted to expand it. Large armies forayed into the southern provinces, even penetrating into what is now Vietnam. One campaign went east, and reached Japan, where some three thousand Chinese eventually settled. To do so, they would have needed sturdy ships, capable of handling the one hundred mile crossing from Korea to Japan across the East China Sea.

Again, there are no representations of these vessels, nor is there any mention in contemporary literature other than a vague reference to an expedition that reached "the three fairy Isles of the Blest." But in 1974, workers digging the foundations of a new office building in Guangzhou discovered first the remnants of a two-thousand-year-old palace, and below that a number of heavy timber beams, each some two-hundred-and-fifty feet long, supported by rows of wooden sleepers.

Little is known about Chinese seafaring during the early dynasties. But recent excavation, often the result of massive construction projects, has begun to unearth valuable evidence (right).

Archaeologists determined that the workers had unearthed a Qin dynasty ship-building site, capable of building and launching several vessels at a time. The size of the berths indicated that the vessels would have measured from thirty-three to one hundred feet in length, and up to twenty-five feet in width. Among the materials found near the site were nails and tools and a wooden device to bend timbers under heat. This made clear that the ships built there twenty-two hundred years earlier were relatively sophisticated, made with long planks bent into shape, and nailed together, rather than fastened with ropes or leather. The current thinking is that they were used for military purposes.

Ships of this size and structure would have been able to reach Japan, as Chinese vessels clearly did during that era. Presumably they would also have been able to reach much of Southeast Asia and even beyond, but of that, as of so much else, no one is certain. On the one hand, there is evidence like that unearthed in Guangzhou, which suggests the construction of sturdy, seaworthy vessels. On the other, there are hardly any references in art or literature to show us what these vessels looked like, or to indicate where they went.

In spite of its importance, the Qin dynasty was short-lived. Following the death of Qin Shihuangdi, the Great Unifier, the empire began to crumble. Amid the subsequent confusion, rebel Liu Bang seized power. He became Han Gao Zu, founder of

the Han dynasty. The Han era was divided into two periods of roughly two hundred years: the first or Western Han dynasty (221 B.C. to 9 A.D.) and the second or Eastern Han dynasty (A.D. 25 to 220). Between the two, the regent Wang Mang briefly ruled the country as the first (and only) Xin emperor.

During the earlier Han period, and particularly during the reign of the emperor Han Wudi (140 to 87 B.C.), China was a well-administered, stable state. Though the empire, as always, was threatened by the Huns north of the Great Wall, the Chinese were interested in contacts with other countries. This led to visits from Syrian traders, who possibly came by sea, but China also made outreach efforts. During Wudi's reign, for instance, a diplomatic mission to seek allies against the Huns made it all the way to Bactria in present-day Afghanistan. Through these efforts, Chinese emissaries not only reached the Greek empire's eastern fringe, but also laid the foundation for the overland Silk Road that linked China with Central Asia and the West.

Wudi is known to have sent maritime expeditions into the Eastern Ocean, but there are no visual representations or reliable literary sources describing the voyages. In fact, to see any representation of a ship at all, we have to wait until the later Han dynasty, when pictures of small boats show up in several stone carvings. One shows people in sampans engaged in peaceful activities; in the other sampans are being used for hostile purposes. These are very small craft, however, with no resemblance to the type of vessels needed to cross the East China Sea to Japan or the South China Sea to Southeast Asia.

Throughout the later Han dynasty, China continued to expand. By the end of the first century its influence reached as far west as the Caspian Sea, and only Parthia in northern Iran separated the Roman and Chinese empires. To protect their sovereignty over this enormous territory, the Han emperors implemented the tributary system, a practice of elaborate rituals designed to keep the barbarian tribes along the borders under

control. The tributaries were expected to send gifts and acknowledge the Chinese emperor as the "ruler of all mankind," in return for which they received gifts and imperial protection.

Trade with tributaries and foreign countries increased, especially with Arabia and Syria by way of India. Whether or not Chinese ships conducted it is not known, though there are many literary references to suggest that some junks ventured as far as India. The dynasty's chronicles *(Han Shu)* describe Han trade with the South Seas and mention that the furthest country took twelve months to reach—plenty of time to bring even a very slow ship as far as the western rim of the Indian Ocean. The book also mentions Huang-chih, a destination unknown today. Conservative estimates place it near modern-day Conjeeveram (Kanchipuram) on the Indian Malabar coast, but it could also have been the port of Adulis (Massawa) on the Red Sea. If this were the case, Chinese sailors could have reached East Africa as early as Han times.

Aside from the literary record, there is also some interesting archaeological evidence. In the late 1950s, for instance, a number of pottery ship models were discovered in Han tombs near Guangzhou. Though relatively coarse, these are the first actual representations of Chinese ships and they show quite advanced vessels, with several masts, watertight bulkheads and, most importantly, a stern rudder—proof that rudders were known in China since Han times, if not earlier. In Europe and elsewhere, sailors would continue to use steering oars for at least another thousand years.

The Han Dynasty chronicles claim that Chinese vessels sailed to the Indian Malabar coast as early as 2,000 years ago. But whether there was a Chinese maritime presence here at that stage is not yet clear.

The Chinese meanwhile had developed the stern rudder into an efficient steering device. The rudder on some Han ship models is already balanced, for instance, with part of the blade forward of the post. This not only reduced the weight on the bearings, it also eased the workload of the helmsman. Chinese mariners also found out that steering was much easier if the rudder was riddled with holes, which led to the development of the fenestrated rudder. The holes, usually diamond-shaped, reduced the pressure against the rudder blade, and did so without reducing its efficiency.

Without chance finds like these tomb models, we would not know for certain when the Chinese invented something as essential as the stern rudder. In Western civilizations the artistic or literary record would have revealed a similar development, but it appears that Chinese artists and writers were not very nautically minded. Other than some tomb reliefs, sculptors produced little of maritime interest. There are hardly any drawings or paintings with ships from Han times either. In subsequent dynasties original works showing sampans and junks were occasionally produced, but few of these reveal anything new. For one thing, Chinese artists confined themselves to painting ships on rivers and lakes; a picture of a seagoing junk is quite rare. In addition, few pictures show any nautical detail. Chinese artists did not draw boats for the sake of boats until much later. They drew them because a philosopher or high official happened to be meditating nearby, or because they were part of a landscape.

Chinese literature of this period provides more information, but unfortunately much of it is not very specific or even instructive. For instance, several accounts dating back to Han times are replete with references to great maritime exploits, but they fail to mention who achieved them. There also is no visual record to back up any of these claims, or at least show what the ships looked like. Understandably then, one threads carefully through China's literary references, trying to strike a balance between claims of daring voyages and a remarkable lack of visual evidence.

The Hanshan temple in Suzhou. During the Tang dynasty (A.D. 618 - 907) China considered itself the center of the civilized world.

NEW DYNASTIES

By the end of the second century, the Han emperors' control over their immense empire began to crumble. Political infighting among court factions led to a number of palace revolutions, and in A.D. 220 the government collapsed. China entered a period of instability that would last nearly four hundred years.

Much of the country was ruled at one time or another by a number of warring nations, beginning with the Three Kingdoms, whose battles became legendary. In Luo Guanzhong's celebrated *Romance of the Three Kingdoms*, we are given a tantalizing glimpse of the ships that were supposedly sailing Chinese waters at that time. The book is replete with references to squadrons of fast fighting ships, transport ships, and a sophisticated level of naval warfare that included the use of bombs and fire rafts. There are no descriptions of the type of ships that were involved in these confrontations, which would have been difficult anyway since the book was written so much later. So while it implies that naval power in China during the third century was technically far advanced over anything that existed elsewhere, that assertion has to be taken with a grain of salt. Luo did not necessarily have access to more reliable information than today's historians.

CHINESE SHIPBUILDING: LEARNING FROM NATURE

'To construct a boat, the bottom must be laid first. Along its side the bottom walls are erected, which touch the bottom at the lower end and support the planking of the hull above. Bulkheads are placed at regular intervals to divide the vessel. The part that rises vertically on the side is the hull.'

Song Yingxing wrote these words in 1637 in *The Creations of Nature and Man,* a seventeenth-century encyclopedia of Chinese industrial technology. Though by no means the only such work, this book is particularly interesting because Song took a broad look at Chinese technology from a layman's perspective.

Song's simple description of the construction of a junk confirms that Chinese shipbuilding had a pattern entirely its own. Fundamental to the Chinese approach was the transverse bulkhead, which Song describes as one of the first steps in the junk's construction. Tradition holds that the Chinese derived the idea from the structure of bamboo.

Aside from watertight compartments, other aspects of ship construction were uniquely Chinese. Nearly everywhere, the first step was the laying down of the keel, with the stempost and the stern-post attached at either end. But not in China. The vessels that Song describes did not have a stem- and stern-post, or even a keel. They had a flat or slightly rounded bottom. Their planking did not curve to close toward stem and stern, but instead ended abruptly in solid transoms of straight planks. Vessels like this still operate on China's Tai Lake (Tai Hu), though recently the trend has been to use hulls made from ferro-cement rather than wood.

Oceangoing vessels needed the more rigid construction provided by a keel, a structure that began to appear on Chinese vessels by the Song Dynasty. In fact, the population movement southward may well have had something to do with changes in shipbuilding technology, because southern waters required different ships. Here the coast was deeply indented, but also more exposed. North of the Yangtze River, in contrast, the sea was shallower, with shoals and sandbars sometimes stretching for some miles out. For those waters, the flat-bottomed junk with bluff bows described by Song was ideal; in the south, a ship with keel, sharper bow, and deeper draft did better. Nonetheless, keel-less ships also made long ocean-crossings, as is clear from the appearance of *sha chuan* or sand-ships in Nagasaki in the eighteenth century (see: The *Tōsen no Zu,* p. 106). To help these flat-bottomed estuarine vessels maintain a course against contrary winds, shipbuilders outfitted them with leeboards.

To the Western eye, the average junk, with its low stem and high stern, was not always aesthetically pleasing. In comparison to the European and American clippers that called at Chinese ports during the nineteenth century, some junks looked downright bulky and unwieldy, and Western observers often resorted to unflattering descriptions of China's nautical technology. But they failed to take into account the nature of a vessel that had remained unchanged for hundreds of years. When the junk reached its peak, from the twelfth through the early fifteenth centuries, it was more advanced in many respects than most Western vessels.

Song's description is invaluable for yet another reason. He does not mention plans or blueprints. Chinese shipbuilders constructed their vessels without any of these, or even a sketch of the ship's design. They relied, as did their fathers before and their sons after them, on tradition, skill, and a sense of shape and form. Though the number of traditional boatyards is rapidly dwindling, junks are still built in this way in China. While a remarkable tribute to tradition, this practice means that there are no plans to show us what past vessels might have looked like. Once a ship is gone, it is gone forever. This explains why so much of China's maritime history, from its dim roots to the recent past, remains a matter of frustrating uncertainty and speculation.

Between A.D. 304 to 535 no fewer than seventeen dynasties vied for power in the Middle Kingdom. Several were barbarian, established by invaders that broke through the northern defensive barriers and poured into China. But these successive waves of invaders never threatened Chinese culture or society, as they might have elsewhere. The Chinese peasant was no match for the swiftly attacking hordes from the north, but the invaders, in turn, were no match for the well-organized administrative system they found already in place. Lacking a strong organizational heritage, most were integrated and eventually sinicized.

As a result Chinese civilization did not suffer massive disruptions in its ways of doing things, as might have been expected from such a period of turmoil. Science and culture continued to mature, rather than stagnate. Great progress was made in the sciences of geography, mathematics, and alchemy, and some of China's finest labor saving devices, like the water mill and wheelbarrow, were introduced at that time.

Towards the end of the sixth century, China was united again—this time by Yang Jian, founder of the Sui dynasty. The Sui emperors began extraordinary public works, including the construction of the Grand Canal, an inland waterway designed to connect the northern and southern parts of the country. Millions of people were forced to work on it, and millions perished. The project would be a blessing to later generations, but it proved the Sui dynasty's undoing. Its cost, along with that of military campaigns into Korea and Central Asia, depleted the treasury and created public unrest. In the

The Grand Canal near Wuxi. More than 1,200 miles long, it developed into a commercial artery linking North and South. But the high cost of construction, in lives as well as in funds, caused the collapse of the Sui dynasty.

midst of the confusion Li Yuan, an official, seized power. A year later, in A.D. 618, he proclaimed the Tang dynasty.

For the next three hundred years Tang emperors would rule and expand an empire that justifiably claimed to be the center of the civilized world. As during Han times, the Tang Chinese welcomed foreigners, and Xian (Chang'an), their capital, became an international meeting place. Arab traders were accommodated when they arrived in China in 787, as Indians, Syrians, and Persians had been before. Along with this influx of foreign cultures came new practices and ideas, including novel religions like Islam and Christianity. The arts flourished and there were important technological advances, including printing and the manufacture of ceramics.

Unfortunately so little is known about China's maritime doings at this time that historians refer to it as a "blank period." It is clear that Persian and Arab vessels called at Chinese ports, but whether Chinese vessels also ventured across the Indian Ocean seems doubtful. There were accounts of Chinese travelers heading towards distant lands, but few, if any, ever mention taking passage on Chinese ships. References to Indian, Arab, and Persian ships, on the other hand, abound, indicating that China's sea trade probably took place under the aegis of these nations. One late-eighth-century account reports that "the sea-going junks are foreign ships"; they called at Canton (Guangzhou) and An'i. It further mentions that the ships from Ceylon were the largest, with "companion-ways alone being several tens of feet high."

Even though the Tang Chinese may not have been very ocean-oriented, they continued to develop their inland waterways and the ships associated with them. Several texts indicate that naval technologies also continued to improve. A seventh century chronicle talks of fighting ships with as many as five decks that could reportedly carry more than eight hundred sailors and soldiers. Two hundred years later, the Tang Navy had developed several classes of specialized naval vessels, including strengthened, multi-decked battleships known as tower-ships; combat-junks; converted merchantmen known as seahawk-ships; and patrol boats. In the West, this type of naval specialization did not occur until seven hundred and fifty years later.

Yet in spite of such tales of advanced naval technologies and references to well-organized inland shipping, nothing indicates that the Tang Chinese were taking to the oceans in an organized manner. Presumably they conducted commerce in their own ships with other territories in East Asia and Southeast Asia, but the lack of records, ships, or other evidence rules out any certainty.

The massive population move towards southern China and its indented coast caused China to gradually adopt more of a maritime attitude during the Song dynasty.

THE SONG AND MONGOL DYNASTIES

By the late ninth century, the power of the Tang dynasty was dissipating and China was again partitioned. A period of great upheaval followed, with nine or ten independent kingdoms vying for control. It ended in A.D. 960 when Zhao Kuangyin staged a successful military coup and established the Song dynasty, which reunified the country once more.

Zhao immediately set about consolidating his position, bribing both possible contenders for power and the barbarian tribes in the north. A period of peace and stability followed, until the Tartars invaded northern China in 1126, capturing the emperor and virtually the entire government at the capital of Kaifeng. To escape Tartar rule, many Chinese fled to the south. In Hangzhou they established a new capital and government, which became known as the Southern Song.

During Song times, the Chinese began to take a greater interest in the sea. The massive population movements from northern to southern China undoubtedly were a factor, as was the status of the new capital as both a port and the terminal of the Grand Canal. From here the Song Chinese began to control the southern coast, which they found suitable for the development of maritime transport. Unlike the northern coast it was indented with natural harbors and fringed with thousands of small islands that provided not only excellent anchorages but also some of China's finest forests, needed for the building of large seagoing vessels.

Along with this gradual turn to the sea came more accurate records of China's maritime activities. In contrast to the "blank period" of Tang times, a veritable profusion of records, travel tales, and even paintings emerges, depicting the ships and shipping of that period. They make clear that shipbuilding techniques improved and that large, multiple-masted junks were being constructed. These ships, in turn, were for the first time equipped with a Chinese invention that would make long voyages safer and vastly more practical: the compass (see p. 100). And more ships inevitably led to a greater number of wrecks, some of which have now been excavated, shedding additional light on the maritime technology of Song China.

The Southern Song dynasty did not retain its control of southern China for long. Early in the twelfth century the Tartars, who had driven the Song out of northern China, were in turn overrun by the Mongol hordes of Genghis Khan. In 1215 Beijing was taken, Kaifeng followed in 1233, and by 1234 the Mongols were attacking the borders of Song-controlled China, eager to add it to their growing territory. It took them nearly fifty years to do so. In 1279 the last Song prince was killed in a terrible sea battle at Yaishan near Guangzhou, and at long last the Mongols could claim to rule all of China.

During their hundred-year reign, the Mongol or Yuan emperors controlled the largest empire the world had ever known, stretching from Beijing to Budapest in the north and from Guangzhou to Basra in the south. Still, Kublai Khan, grandson of Genghis Khan and the first Yuan ruler, was determined to further expand this immense territory. Early in his reign, he set his mind on the conquest of Japan. When he sent a mission across the Sea of Japan to invite the Japanese emperor to surrender to Mongol suzerainty, the ruling Hōjō regency sent it back empty-handed. In fact, to add insult to injury, the principal emissaries were beheaded. War then became inevitable.

The Mongols were understandably not much of a seafaring nation, but in their naval battles with the Song Chinese they had performed surprisingly well. Now they mustered all their strength and experience for their greatest naval venture yet: the invasion of Japan. Late in 1274 a fleet numbering over nine hundred junks set sail from Mongol-controlled Korea. It carried twenty-five thousand Mongols and their horses and fifteen thousand Korean troops. The invasion force landed near Hakata Bay on the island of Kyushu, disembarked, and prepared to take the fortified town of Hakata, its capital. But a gath-

Kublai Khan had his eyes set on Japan, a former ally of the Song Chinese. The subsequent Mongol invasions of the country cost tens of thousands of lives.

ering storm forced the Mongols to return to their ships to ride out the weather. It proved a disaster. Heavily battered, the fleet limped back to Korea. One-third of the invasion force had either drowned in the storm or been killed on the island.

The campaign against the Song Chinese diverted Kublai Khan's naval resources, but after finally eliminating the last remnants of opposition in 1279, Kublai turned his gaze eastward once more. That same year, he ordered the construction of 1,500 war junks. Two years later he added several thousand more. Along the Korean and Chinese coasts, the Mongols were amassing the largest fleet the world had ever seen. When the Japanese got word of this gargantuan effort, they set about building ships of their own and fortifying their coastal defenses. Around the town of Hakata they erected a massive wall, eight feet high and nearly twelve miles long. It would prove a wise investment.

In the spring of 1281, the invasion fleet was ready. From Pusan in Korea a fleet of a thousand ships and forty-two thousand men set sail, intending to meet at sea with a Chinese contingent of thirty-five hundred junks and more than one hundred thousand troops. Both fleets met at the island of Iki, where they annihilated the local defenders. They then proceeded to Hakata Bay, where they had landed seven years earlier.

The wall around Hakata robbed the Mongol invasion force of its fearsome cavalry charge, and for seven weeks the two armies were locked in combat, with the Mongols only gradually gaining ground. But in August a massive typhoon struck Kyushu. No ship could withstand such fury and the invasion fleet was destroyed at its

THE MARINER'S COMPASS: A CHINESE INVENTION

Like sailors in other regions, the Chinese relied on a variety of clues to find their way at sea. They observed winds and currents, took bottom samples, and noted landmarks and other characteristics of coastal areas that could help them determine their position. But once out of sight of land, navigation became a different matter. To figure out where they were on the open sea, the Chinese used the sun, the moon, and the stars. Clearly they excelled at observation of the night sky. "There are in all 2,500 greater stars, not including the ones which the sea people observe," wrote the great astronomer Zhang Heng during Han times in A.D. 118. This pool of knowledge enabled navigators to obtain some idea of their latitude by observing the rising and setting of a number of stars, and by measuring the position of the pole star above the horizon.

Nonetheless, as elsewhere, these methods led to no more than rough position estimates because it was impossible to tell time and distance with any degree of precision. Though the results were usually acceptable for short distances in well-known waters, the lack of accuracy could be a major problem during long ocean crossings, especially on overcast days when no sun or stars could be observed. The introduction of the compass at sea during the eleventh century represented an important step in reducing this uncertainty.

Interestingly, the Chinese took a remarkably long time to make this step. By Song times, spoon-shaped objects of lodestone, which rotated on a bronze plate, had existed for at least a thousand years. But these devices were not necessarily used to hold to a particular direction. Instead, the Chinese believed that "south-controlling spoons," as they were known, were most useful in conjunction with prognostication and divination; for instance, in finding out how particular phenomena might affect the health and welfare of the Middle Kingdom and its ruler. They did not recognize the mysterious "south-pointer" as a direction-finding instrument until much later, and even then they used it more often to maintain a mystical harmony between man and his surroundings than to keep to a given course.

Sailors needed a compass that would function on a moving platform, and this called for something different than a spoon rotating on a plate. They found that they could achieve the same effect with a magnetized needle floating on water in a small cup. The first mention of a device of this sort, which dates back to 1044, describes the "south-pointing fish" as a leaf-like piece of magnetized iron floating on water. Chinese sailors remained faithful to these relatively simple devices for hundreds of years.

From the late eleventh century on, compasses began to appear regularly aboard ships. "Magicians rub the point of a needle with a lodestone," wrote Shen Kua in 1080, "after which it is able to point to the south." He also described declination: "but it always inclines slightly to the east, and does not point directly south." Zhu Yu, referring to navigation during the late eleventh century, wrote that pilots "steer by the stars at night, and in the day time by the sun; in dark weather they look at the south-pointing needle."

Before long navigation without a compass became unthinkable, as the literary record shows: "This has to be watched day and night with attention," Zhan Juxua wrote in his *Records of Foreign Peoples*, "for life or death will depend on the slightest fraction of error." Another source is even more poetic: "The water of the ocean is shallow near islands and reefs—if a reef is struck the whole ship may well be lost. This depends entirely on the compass needle, and if a small mistake is made you will be buried in the body of a shark."

anchorage. A total of four thousand ships sank. More than one hundred thousand troops were either drowned or massacred when they tried to crawl ashore. The remainder returned to China, defeated by the elements a second time.

The Great Khan never attempted an invasion of Japan again, though he did not lose his taste for conquest or even his faith in naval power. From 1283 through 1289, he directed a series of naval campaigns against Annam in today's Vietnam. And in 1292, he sent a fleet of a thousand junks to strike Java in Indonesia. Until his death in 1294, Kublai Khan contemplated a third Japanese invasion attempt; but his plan met with public resistance and never materialized. The Japanese, for their part, believed that the gods had sent the typhoon in answer to their prayers. They came to know it as *kamikaze*—the divine wind. It confirmed their belief that Japan was sacred soil, and that it was the gods' intent to preserve and protect it.

Despite the Yuan dynasty's interest in naval and maritime matters, its chroniclers have little to tell us about their ships. None wrote about the merchant junks of that time; they simply did not seem worth mentioning, even though old sea routes were reestablished and sea trade grew in importance.

Fortunately, there are other reliable sources. With much of Central Asia under Mongol control, travel to and from the West became much safer, and several Europeans and Muslims seized the opportunity to visit the Middle Kingdom. Marco Polo, the most famous among them, spent nearly seventeen years in China as a court official. To him we owe the first Western glimpses of Yuan China, including its maritime activities.

Marco Polo wrote at length about Chinese ships and shipping. Describing the Chinese custom of building junks with watertight bulkheads, he noted the considerable safety benefits of this technique: "if by accident the ship is staved in any place ... then the water through the whole runs to the bilge ... And then the sailors find out where the ship is staved, and then the hold which answers to the break is emptied into others, for the water cannot pass from one hold to another, so strongly are they shut in; and then they repair the ship there, and put back there the goods which had been taken out." In spite of his clear description, European shipbuilders did not adopt this technique until hundreds of years later. Thousands of ships and innumerable lives would have been saved if they had.

Polo and other European travelers were also impressed with the number of masts on Chinese vessels. Some junks, he noted, have "four masts and four sails and they often add to them two masts more, which are raised and put away every time they wish." He also described the "great ships in which the merchants come and go through the Indian Sea," adding that, on deck, "there are commonly in all 60 little rooms or cabins ... where in each a merchant can stay comfortably." Polo knew what he was talking about. On his return to the West, he joined a fleet of four-masted junks that sailed from China to the Middle East to take a Mongol princess to the Court of Persia. In that way he experienced China's maritime capabilities firsthand.

Polo's writings are confirmed by later Chinese accounts that speak of fleets that "swept the seas of Java and Malaya" and enormous freighters that carried up to a thousand tons of grain on the ten-day route from Shanghai to Tianjin. "When their sails are spread they are like great clouds in the sky," wrote one chronicler. "There is no going back to the mainland once the people have set forth upon the cerulean sea."

Poetic as this all may sound, it does not provide many details. A more specific account has come down from the great Arab traveler Ibn Battuta, who spent much of the early fourteenth century traveling throughout Asia. Along India's Malabar Coast

101

he found fifteen junks at anchor. His description of these vessels is fascinating: "the greater ships had from three to twelve sails, made of strips of bamboo and woven like mats. Each of them had a crew of 1000 men—600 sailors and 400 soldiers, and had three tenders attached to them…. Each vessel had four decks and numerous private and public cabins for the merchant passengers."

Perhaps some of the numbers are exaggerated, but Battuta's comments at least prove that Chinese ships were regularly sailing to India and beyond. Regardless of their actual size, Western ships of that time would have been hard pressed to match the feat.

The Forbidden City — official residence of most Ming emperors. Its construction was initiated by Zhu Di, the Yongle emperor, known for his ambitious maritime policies.

ZHENG HE AND THE IMPERIAL FLEET

Though the Yuan emperors adopted the Chinese way of running and administering the country, they never succeeded in adequately controlling its bureaucracy. Perhaps this was a result of their distrust of the Chinese who, although they were recruited for the government, never received high posts. Naturally this created a good deal of resentment against the Mongol overlords.

By the middle of the fourteenth century, the days of the Yuan dynasty were numbered. An increasing number of active rebel groups succeeded in defeating Mongol-backed forces. As in the previous change of power, naval battles played a crucial role. In 1356, for instance, a rebel fleet soundly defeated its Mongol counterpart with guns and mortars at Anhui. Six years later, the two fleets met in the battle of Jiangxi with similar results. An eyewitness account speaks of sounds like thunder, towering waves, the "flare of the flying fire," and the water turning red. Jiangxi sealed the fate of the Mongol fleet and the Yuan dynasty.

The leader of the naval battles at Jiangxi and Anhui, and of the capture of Nanjing and Beijing in 1366, was Zhu Yuanzhang, an orphaned peasant who had risen through the rebel ranks. In 1368 Zhu, who emerged as the rebels' sole leader, established the Ming dynasty, and became its first emperor. He established his court in Nanjing.

With the Mongols only recently defeated, Zhu set about consolidating China's defenses and driving the remaining Mongol units out of the country. He also ordered massive irrigation projects and an extensive reconstruction of the canal system. But the first Ming emperor did not share the openness towards foreigners of his predecessors. Though he was keen to reestablish the tributary system, he did not permit the Chinese themselves to go overseas. Anyone that did so was to be executed as a traitor. In 1374, he even abolished the merchant ship organizations in China's major ports. The country's sea trade inevitably declined.

Even so this interruption in the Middle Kingdom's dawning maritime ambitions was relatively short-lived. Zhu's death in 1398 threw the country into a bitterly fought struggle for control. Eventually Zhu's fourth son, Zhu Di, emerged victorious. As third Ming emperor he took on the name Yongle, and moved the capital back to Beijing.

Yongle was as keen as his father to further the tributary system, but he had different ideas on how to achieve this. China needed a large navy, he believed, to convince other states of its supremacy. A large navy could also help curtail the growing threat of piracy along its southern coast. Accordingly he called for a massive expansion in China's sea power. By 1403 China was building large numbers of seagoing junks to implement these plans. Two years later, the first of seven enormous naval expeditions left China for the "Western Ocean."

The few surviving fragments of this impressive maritime deployment are truly astounding. During a thirty-year period, no less than seven expeditions ventured to places as far as the East Coast of Africa, the Red Sea, the Persian Gulf, India, and Southeast Asia. Each expedition involved thousands of men and hundreds of ships, among them the largest and most advanced ships in the world.

In command of the voyages was Zheng He, China's most famous and capable sea commander. Born around 1371, Zheng He grew up in Yunnan province in a Muslim family. In 1382, during the final rout of the Mongols, he and his family were taken prisoner. As was customary at the time, the boy was castrated; he then entered into the service of Zhu Di, the emperor's fourth son, who would later become emperor.

Zheng He distinguished himself during Zhu Di's successful grab for power, and in 1404, in a show of imperial favor, he was made superintendent of the office of eunuchs. But he did not stay there for long. The emperor realized that Zheng He's diplomatic and military skills, and his knowledge of Turku and Islam, made him uniquely qualified to command naval expeditions. Accordingly he was appointed commander in chief of the Ming Fleet the following year.

Aside from this, little is known about Zheng He. Most accounts describe him as a man of remarkable character and appearance, who was tall and strong. Naturally they expound upon his virtues as a diplomat, commander, and strategist. As China's foremost maritime traveler, he quickly attained near-legendary status. Even sober historians accepted the fact that he was reported to be at least nine feet tall. It appears he simply was taller than life.

Zheng He oversaw the preparations for the first expedition, which left Nanjing in 1405 with a force of more than 27,000 men aboard 317 ships. Among these were sixty-two *baochuan* or treasure ships, so called because they carried "unnamed treasures of untold quantities." These were the largest ships constructed by the Chinese, or anyone else for that matter. Ming records mention a length of forty-four *chang*—nearly 440 feet—and nine masts, but this may be an overestimate. Nautical experts believe the vessels would have measured a maximum of 300 feet and 3,000 tons, which was still considerably larger than any European ship. Aside from the treasure ships, the fleet also included troop carriers, supply ships, and water carriers of various sizes. The large number of vessels suggests that on several occasions ships were dispatched from the main fleet for exploratory voyages.

According to the records of the first voyage, Zheng He visited Indonesia and Sri Lanka before heading on to Quilon and Calicut in India, where he received tributes and acknowledgments from local rulers. On the return voyage, the Chinese fleet defeated the forces of Chen Tsui, a notorious Chinese pirate chief who operated out of Palembang in Sumatra. Zheng He's men killed some five thousand of his cronies, and returned the captured Chen Tsui to Nanjing, where he was executed. Delayed by this action, the fleet did not return to China until the fall of 1407.

Zheng He did not accompany the second expedition, though he was its official commander. This time a fleet of 249 ships and an unknown number of men headed back towards Calicut, calling at Thailand, Java, and Cochin along the way.

During the fifth voyage, the imperial fleet sailed as far as Pate in northern Kenya. At that time Pate was an important Swahili trade center; today it seldom sees visitors.

The third expedition was ordered to visit "the seas of the west." Consisting of 30,000 men and 48 ships, the fleet left in the fall of 1409, just a few months after the second expedition had returned. The armada called at Champa (Vietnam), Java, Malacca, Semudera, and Sri Lanka before sailing onward to the Indian west coast. On the return voyage, the Chinese fought a series of violent battles with Sinhalese forces off Sri Lanka. After soundly defeating their adversaries, the Chinese fleet set a course for home, returning during the summer of 1411.

In the fall of 1413, a fourth expedition set out. It followed the usual route to the Indian subcontinent, but after calling at Calicut traveled beyond, crossing the western Indian Ocean to Hormuz. Zheng He also received specific instructions to call at northern Sumatra and defeat forces that had rebelled against the rightful king of the area, defined by the Chinese as the ruler who had rendered tribute in previous years. The large Chinese force quickly dealt with the rebels, capturing and executing their leader Sekandar. The expedition returned to China during the summer of 1415.

One of the people accompanying this voyage was Ma Huan, a young interpreter. Ma Huan took extensive notes on the places visited, which he arranged in book form upon his return to China. Since the manuscript survived, we have much more information about this voyage than the ones that preceded it.

The fifth expedition left in the fall of 1417. There is no information on the number of ships and men involved, but we know the principal objective of the voyage was to escort the ambassadors from nineteen countries to their homes and to offer gifts to these rulers in return for their tribute. The ambassadors reportedly came from as far as Mogadishu and Malindi on the African East Coast, and accordingly Zheng He's fleet, for the first time, sailed that far. On the outbound leg, the expedition called at several Southeast Asian countries, as well as Sri Lanka, India, Hormuz, and Aden. The fleet encountered unfriendly receptions at Lasa on the Arabian coast and near Mogadishu, indications that it was not always welcomed. Nonetheless, a display of military force proved sufficient to avoid trouble, and the fleet returned safely to China in the summer of 1419.

Two years later, a fleet of forty-one ships and an unknown number of men followed a similar course to return another group of ambassadors to their countries. The fleet again reached East Africa and the Persian Gulf, though it is doubtful that Zheng He accompanied it that far. It appears that he visited some places in Southeast Asia and then returned to China with part of the fleet, while his subordinates went on to the more distant regions.

Shortly after the return of the sixth fleet in 1424, Yongle died. It appeared an end had come to these ambitious voyages. Yongle's successor, the Hongxi emperor, was not interested in exploration and immediately suspended all overseas expeditions. But his successor, Zhu Zhanji, who became known as the Xuande emperor, ordered one more voyage to the "Western Sea." The fleet set out in 1430, with 27,750 men in 100 ships. It was Zheng He's, and Ming China's, last voyage.

Ma Huan accompanied the journey and left an account, as did Zhu Yunming, who recounted it using contemporary sources about a hundred years later. As a result we know more about this final voyage than any of the others. A detailed itinerary

The imperial shipyards in Nanjing, or rather what is left of them. This is where the great treasure ships were built in the early 15th century. As a result of Nanjing's continuing expansion, the site may vanish forever.

Sometime in the early eighteenth century, probably between 1717 and 1720, Matsuura Atsunobu, the ruler of the small island of Hirado in southern Japan, received an important request from Tokugawa Yoshimune, then the Shōgun of Japan. Why, the Japanese ruler wanted to know, were Chinese ships faster than their Japanese counterparts? And what could be done about it?

Tokugawa Yoshimune was not, as far as we know, very interested in maritime technology. After all, his country had been closed for more than one hundred years. The Japanese were strictly forbidden to voyage overseas, or to even make ships that could undertake overseas voyages. Why this sudden interest in foreign ships?

There was a pragmatic reason for Yoshimune's request. From the early years of the Tokugawa shōgunate, Japan's imports and exports were funneled through one single port: Nagasaki. Every year a few Dutch ships entered Nagasaki harbor, along with a good number of Chinese vessels that, of course, had undertaken a much shorter trip. Dutch and Chinese merchants were strictly isolated from the rest of the Japanese population.

During the early years of the Manchu dynasty, Chinese merchants were relatively free to trade, so a good number of vessels were sent to Nagasaki, bringing silks and porcelain, and seeking to return with silver and copper, which were needed for the casting of coins. But early in the eighteenth century, it became clear that the amount of copper produced in Japan was insufficient to meet Chinese needs. In response, the Japanese government in 1715 imposed strict limitations on the number of Chinese ships that were allowed to enter Nagasaki. At first the number was set to thirty, later to twenty and then just to ten. To control the quota, ships that were allowed to enter Nagasaki were given a permit known as a *shinpai*. Others were told not to come.

Considering that many more Chinese vessels had been sailing to Japan in the years prior to the restrictions, many traders now faced going out of business. But the Chinese were not about to simply give in. They sailed to the islands north of Nagasaki, among them Hirado, and looked for a chance to offload their cargoes illegally. The Japanese authorities tried to prevent this, but their vessels were no match for the Chinese vessels, which hauled anchor and usually got away. And so the Shōgun's request made sense. He wanted to have as much information on Chinese ships as possible so that his own forces could better control them.

A request made by Japan's ruler was not to be taken lightly, and therefore Matsuura Atsunobu commissioned his best artist to draw pictures of Chinese ships and their equipment. Besides providing the shōgunate with the requested information, these pictures left an unparalleled record of Chinese merchant ships of the early eighteenth century. Nothing like this exists in China or anywhere else, with the exception of a similar scroll, probably painted by the same artist, now at the National Gallery of Victoria in Melbourne.

Aside from his evident skill, little is known about the artist. He presented his work in a horizontal scroll known as the *Tōsen no Zu*, almost thirty-three feet long and eleven inches wide. On it he depicted eleven Chinese ships and one Dutch merchantman in exquisite detail and true to scale, which could not be said of the Japanese woodcut artists who sometimes depicted the ships seen in Nagasaki harbor. More important, the artist represented the entire ship, including the hull below the waterline, using vivid colors and high-quality paint. In other words, this was a work suitable for the highest authorities. And it has survived the nearly three hundred years since its completion in perfect condition.

Sha chuan

The first ship depicted on the *Tōsen no Zu* was known in China as *sha chuan* or sand ship. In Nagasaki the ships were called *mame-fune* (bean-ships) or more properly Nanjing ships, which was misleading since they sailed mostly from Shanghai.

This ship is quite different from the other Chinese vessels on the scroll, its prime characteristics being that it is flat-bottomed and without a keel, a design that would have made it more suitable for calm, shallow waters. To improve its sailing ability at sea, it was outfitted with large leeboards on the side that, along with a deep-set rudder, would have kept it from drifting too much when the wind came from the side. As one Japanese observer poetically put it, the leeboards or *waki-kaji* allowed the ships "to fight with the wind."

Unlike the other vessels on the scroll, the hull is stained above the water-line, and the stern is much higher than the bow of the ship—a characteristic of northern Chinese ships, which originated on calm, shallow waters. According to the precise measurements on the scroll, the vessel was about one hundred ten feet long and sixteen feet wide. As is to be expected with a flat-bottomed vessel, it drew little water—only about seven feet.

With favorable winds, the ship could make the passage from the Chinese coast to southern Japan in five days. However, the seas between Shanghai and Nagasaki can be quite rough, and Nanjing ships would not have made for a comfortable passage, especially in large seas.

Chōsen

The next nine Chinese vessels on the *Tōsen no Zu* can be roughly classified as *Chōsen* or bird-ships. On the scroll, they have different names, depending on the port they came from: Ningbo, Guangzhou, and Fuzhou ships get two drawings each, and Taiwan, Calapa (Batavia), and Xiamen (Amoy) vessels, one. In spite of the differing names, all the vessels are quite similar, with black topsides, well-built hulls with a strong keel, and generally three masts, though the mizzenmast seems to be mostly for setting flags. Some of the ships also set a square topsail on the mainmast, which undoubtedly was a Western addition.

As their names indicate, some of these ships covered long distances. Even the ships originating in Fuzhou and Ningbo sometimes went to Southeast Asia to trade there first, and after-

wards set course for Nagasaki with a cargo of local products—a triangle trade that the flat-bottomed sand-ships could never have handled. But all so-called bird ships were clearly built as seagoing ships. They measured an average of one hundred feet, with a beam of between twenty and twenty-five feet, and drew between thirteen and seventeen feet of water.

Siam ship

The final Chinese vessel depicted is also the largest: the Siam ship, so-named because it carried Thai goods to Nagasaki. In spite of its name, this was a Chinese vessel that would have been manned by a Chinese crew, possibly numbering as many as one hundred.

The Siam ship measured nearly one hundred forty feet in length, twenty-six feet in width and had a draft of more than twenty feet, making it considerably larger than the various bird ships. Like the smaller vessels it had three masts, but here the mizzen was actually used to set a sail and flags. And like some of the bird ships it set a square topsail on the mainmast, and in this case a bowsprit sail as well—additions that were copied from Western vessels.

The route from Siam to Nagasaki was probably the longest sea trade route regularly covered during Manchu times. According to Japanese records, the trip would have taken from forty to sixty days. The ships tried to reach Nagasaki by June to avoid the typhoon season, but several accounts describe ships that did not make the port in time and drifted far from their destination as a result of bad weather.

reveals that the passage from Nanjing to Hormuz, including its many stopovers, measured 7,465 miles and required 146 days of sailing. The shorter homeward trip covered 5,740 miles, which took nearly four months. The fleet returned to Nanjing on July 7, 1433, after visiting nineteen countries.

During the thirty years from 1404 to 1433, as the dominant sea power of the Orient, China possessed the most advanced and powerful navy in the world. At is height, the Ming navy numbered 400 major warships stationed at Nanjing, 2,700 warships at the coastal guard stations, 400 armed grain transports, and 250 treasure ships capable of carrying at least 500 men each. But after the return of the seventh voyage, this entire fleet was dismantled. No longer interested in maritime exploration, China's new emperors prohibited it, and the country turned its back on the sea once more. Two years later Zheng He died, and within a generation most Chinese did not even know of his astonishing achievements and adventures.

To understand why China turned so abruptly from its age of maritime dominance, we have to understand why it sent these voyages out in the first place. The Yongle emperor was interested in enhancing China's prestige by an impressive display of naval might, a practice Western nations used (and continue to use) for much the same reasons hundreds of years later. The voyages also helped reestablish China's complicated tribute system. And there probably was some expectation that they would help stimulate the flow of goods to and from the West.

The voyages of the Ming fleets appear to have achieved all this. In the course of the expeditions Zheng He and his men visited more than forty countries, whose rulers sent tributes to the Ming court. The voyages also stimulated trade, which benefited the Chinese treasury. Many of the treasure ships returned loaded with new and exciting goods, among them rare gems and minerals, unknown herbs and drugs, tropical fruits and foods, and exotic animals such as zebras and a giraffe. At the same time, China collected valuable information not only about peoples in other countries, but also about their strengths and capabilities.

Though the expeditions were undoubtedly enormously expensive, it seems that these gains could have offset the costs. But China never undertook these voyages with the intent of merely making money or monopolizing trade. Increased trade with India, Southeast Asia, and Africa was insufficient from the bureaucracy's perspective. What was there to gain other than trade and exotic products?

"Your minister hopes that your majesty ... would not indulge in military pursuits nor glorify the sending of expeditions to distant countries," wrote a high-placed Ming official in 1426, voicing the opinion of many in the court. "Abandon the barren lands abroad and give the people of China a respite so that they can devote themselves to husbandry and to the schools." We have no business overseas, he meant: there is nothing to gain; we should focus on our own concerns. It was a popular doctrine, very Chinese in its own right. China turned its back at a time when it could have ruled the Indian Ocean, believing that it was not profitable, economically or politically.

Other factors also played a role. The reopening of the Grand Canal in 1411, for instance, again permitted the shipment of grain on the inland route. The coastal maritime route lost its importance, and this diversion was soon felt in the maritime community, which had relied heavily on the coastal grain trade. Finally, during the early fifteenth century, China began to regularly experience trouble along its continental borders, particularly in the north. It strengthened its defenses, diverting resources and attention to border security instead of ambitious maritime endeavors.

So it was for pragmatic as well as ideological reasons that China declined to pursue its oceanic ambitions. The resultant destruction of the Ming navy remains one of the greatest tragedies in maritime history. In a matter of years, virtually all of China's maritime know-how was destroyed or forgotten. Official records, including detailed maps and reports of the voyages, were hidden or destroyed, lest others try to repeat the voyages. Before the end of the century, shipbuilders no longer knew how to build the great treasure ships that had sailed the "Western Sea" and impressed its coastal states. In fact, by the early sixteenth century, building a seagoing junk with more than two masts was a capital offense. Coastal officials were required to destroy all such vessels and arrest their crews.

China's maritime decline could not have come at a worse time. Within years, the first European ships would be arriving in Chinese waters. They could not compare with the vessels that had sailed under Zheng He's command a hundred years earlier, but they would quickly make up the differences. For they had come to stay…

DEFEAT AND RESURGENCE

By the middle of the seventeenth century, corruption and internal power struggles were deteriorating the Ming dynasty's power. Into the vacuum stepped the Manchus, a northern tribe that had little interest in maritime matters. Its leaders established China's final dynasty, the Manchu or Qing, which ruled until the Republican Revolution of 1911.

Initially the Qing emperors manifested brief periods of interest in the sea and maritime commerce, but later emperors as a rule followed the policy of *haijin* or maritime interdiction, initiated by the final Ming emperors. Chinese rulers felt safer with continentalism. They believed the population was easier to control if ocean trade and other maritime activities were kept to a minimum.

Inevitably, nautical technology slowed to a snail's pace. China was no longer the place to look for maritime enlightenment. After more than two thousand years, development of the Chinese junk came to a halt. Regarded as perfected, its features became frozen into dogma. This proved fatal. The West's nautical technology was hundreds of years behind when the two cultures met at sea, but China's seemingly insurmountable lead vanished in little more than a lifetime. Driven by commercial and religious motives and a keen interest in technology, Europe rapidly developed and improved its ships. Chinese ships, in contrast, were curtailed by stultifying traditions and their owners' reverence for things ancient. Before long, they could no longer compete.

The end of China's role in maritime history came swiftly. For a period of time, junks held their own in the trade of the Eastern seas. They were still larger and sturdier than many European sailing ships, and there were far more of them in Chinese waters. But as the seventeenth and eighteenth centuries progressed, European vessels became more versatile and maneuverable, and far better armed than any junk. Ironically, it was China's technology that enabled Europe's show of power in its waters. China had invented gunpowder and cannons, watertight compartments, rudders, and many other nautical components essential to the European conquest of the seas. Refined and adapted by Western sailors, these now helped displace the Middle Kingdom from the trade it had called its own for more than a thousand years.

China was first confronted with this show of power when a Portuguese mission attempted to establish a trading post near Guangzhou early in the sixteenth century. The Chinese won this first confrontation and expelled the Portuguese, but not for long. By the middle of the century the Portuguese were back, and this time managed to establish a permanent trading base in Macau.

During the seventeenth century the Dutch reached Chinese waters with their powerful East Indiamen, and by the middle of the century so did the English. For some time, China and England traded peacefully in Southeast Asian waters, but the vast surplus of trade from China to the West, caused by a lack of Chinese interest in Western goods, led to the English importing opium from India to reduce the trade deficit. However despicable the practice, there was little China could do. It was powerless against the technological and maritime might of England. Nothing demonstrated China's demise as vividly as the engagements between English warships and Chinese war junks during the ensuing Opium Wars. Chinese vessels sailed bravely into the conflict, but with weaponry that was outdated and inferior, they were annihilated. With them went the stagnant, dying empire they were trying to defend.

China's reverence for tradition, and its distrust of ideas and novelties that could upset a delicate balance, soon relegated the junk to obscurity. It no longer played a role in international trade. But it did not disappear from the world's seas altogether. Ironically, the country's desire to cling to the established order gave the junk a reprieve. Many Chinese saw no reason to do away with a proven design, and for this reason some of China's inland and coastal trade was, and still is, carried in junks.

Modern junks have adopted some of the West's ideas, including the more maneuverable bow of Western ships, but enough remains of the design of centuries past that the basic shape of junks can be recognized even in the most recent, motorized ships. Sail-driven junks also still exist, though along the coast they have become a very

rare sight. Most survive on inland lakes, where declining fish catches have imposed capacity-limiting regulations, such as forcing a ship to fish under sail. This situation creates an artificial way of keeping junks afloat, but is a tribute to the resilience of the junk. After all, the ships that eventually forced junks out of the main Asian trades are no longer at work. The few that survive train young people in the ways of the sea, or have been permanently docked, serving as reminders of days long gone.

In China, there is no need to visit a museum to see maritime history. In every port and on every river the descendants of one of the most successful vessels in history can still be found, carrying goods or retrieving the sea's bounty. In comparison to their modern counterparts they may look insignificant, but this is deceptive. These ships once ruled much of Asia, and for a brief time seas far beyond. Most important, they represented the maritime technology of one of the world's most advanced cultures, which produced ideas that spread throughout the world, and proved essential to the conquest of the seas.

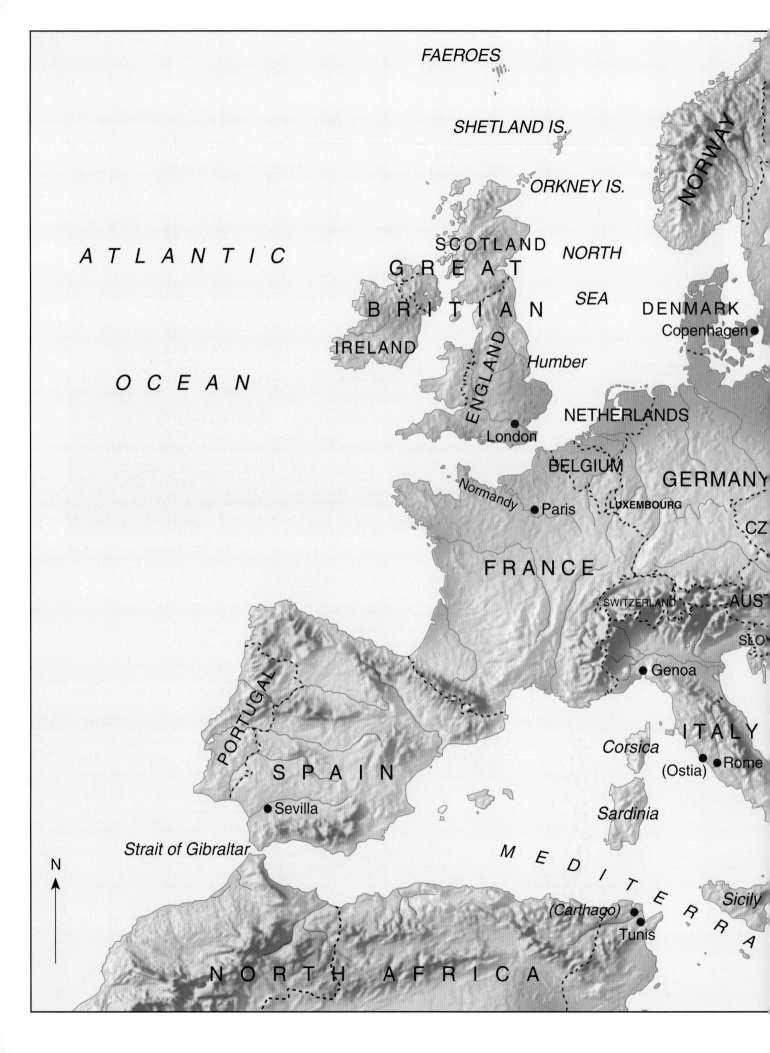

WOODEN SHIPS AND IRON MEN

Life in northern Europe changed dramatically ten thousand years ago. As the last Ice Age ended, the effects of the planet's warming rapidly became noticeable. Temperatures rose and the area's extensive ice cover retreated. Life became somewhat less harsh, but the melting ice cover caused sea levels to rise, inundating low-lying regions and forcing people to move. Along the continent's western edge, a vast expanse filled with water and became the North Sea. Britain became separated from the remainder of the continent, as did the Orkney and Shetland Isles, and countless islands in Scandinavian waters. For the people living there, boats and rafts became indispensable.

The first pictures of boats anywhere date from this time. Cave paintings from Norway and Russia, now estimated to be eleven thousand years old, show the craft of people who lived in northern Europe at the end of the last Ice Age. Probably fashioned from skins stretched over a frame, these boats aided hunters in their pursuit of deer and other game as the animals tried to escape across rivers or lakes.

These were not the first boats; they are simply the first ones we know of with certainty. People in this region began using boats and rafts much earlier. To reach Europe from Africa their ancestors had crossed the Mediterranean at Gibraltar—a feat they achieved on log floats as much as half-a-million years earlier. Eventually their descendants developed dugouts from these floats, but we do not know when this happened. Nothing from that distant age has survived.

But the retreat of the ice cap and the resulting rise in sea level seem to have triggered a flurry of activity, with some remains pointing to an emerging maritime

Sea levels rose throughout northern Europe at the end of the last Ice Age. For the people living here, boats and rafts became indispensable.

technology. In some cases the evidence consists of no more than piles of bones from deep-sea fish, found in or near cave dwellings in Sweden and Scotland. Though not much, they imply that people living there were venturing out to sea as early as the sixth millennium B.C. Elsewhere the remnants include wooden artifacts, thought to be paddles, or hollowed-out tree logs dating back more than eight thousand years. This evidence proves that Neolithic people in northern Europe were consciously building boats, either for fishing and hunting, or for transportation.

By the second millennium B.C., these people had acquired the skills needed to construct more advanced craft, including planked boats. Unlike people in the thriving civilizations of the Near East, they lacked the ability to leave written records to tell us what they did with them, but we know that around this time cattle were introduced to Britain from the continent—an activity that would have required fairly sturdy boats. Similarly, trade products like amber from the Baltic or flint stone from Ulster have been found in Britain, suggesting that a sea trade of sorts between the British Isles and the continent began to develop at this time.

A number of boats from this era were buried under fine sediments, which sealed off the remains and preserved them. Unfortunately, only heavy materials like logs and planks survived the long burial, giving the impression that Bronze Age northern Europeans used mostly wooden boats, which may or may not be true. Nonetheless there is something to be learned from the remains. It was calculated, for instance, that one log canoe, excavated in Britain and found to be nearly three thousand years old, could carry a crew of twenty-eight. Even with a full complement, the vessel's draft was no more than a little over a foot, so that it needed little water. Its ability to carry cargo showed it to be a remarkably efficient vessel.

Europe's oldest known planked boats also come from this area. Their remains were found at North Ferriby in Yorkshire, on a tidal plain of the River Humber. Excavated during the 1930s and '40s, they date back to the middle of the second millennium B.C. Though only a few of the bottom planks were left, archaeologists estimated that the vessels were probably some fifty feet in length, with the planks and side strakes sewn together and made watertight by a caulking of moss. Judging from their most likely original shape, these vessels were probably used as ferries in and around the Humber estuary more than thirty-five hundred years ago.

AEGEANS AND MINOANS

Further south, in the Mediterranean, Neolithic people ventured out to sea as well. They needed obsidian to fashion sharp-edged implements like arrowheads and knives. To obtain it they had to make the crossing from Greece to the island of Melos, something they did at least ten thousand years ago. We do not know what kinds of boats or rafts they used, for they left no visual clues. But we are certain they sailed to Melos because they left the obsidian collected there in their cave dwellings on the mainland.

The documented history of Western seafaring begins in this region. Though none of the earliest ships have been found, sufficient pictures and accounts exist to show that people along the Mediterranean seaboard not only used relatively advanced craft, but also served regular trade routes. Many advanced nautical skills were pioneered by the people of the Aegean—the first great seafarers of Western antiquity.

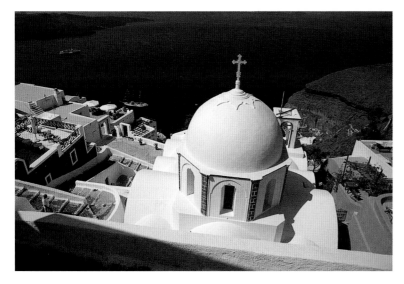

Unlike the Egyptians and Mesopotamians—or even the Chinese, who learned to sail and navigate on rivers—the Aegean islanders were true blue-water sailors. There were no navigable rivers on their islands. From their ports they sailed into open seas instead, probably as early as the third millennium B.C. By the time the Ferriby people in Britain were cautiously poling their goods across the Humber, the Aegean islanders were trading across much of the eastern Mediterranean.

Long-distance sea trade developed in response to certain needs or opportunities, which the flourishing of Minoan civilization on Crete provided. Minoan products have been found along the central and eastern Mediterranean, indicating that these goods were widely distributed and probably highly sought after. In fact, it appears that the Minoans operated a service economy, importing raw materials and fashioning them into anything from exquisite jewelry to everyday utensils. They loaded these products aboard ships and transported them north as far as Macedonia, south to Egypt and North Africa, and east to the countries of the Levant and Asia Minor. The ships sailed westward as far as Sardinia and perhaps even the coast of Spain. On the return trips

The Aegean island of Thera. On the sea routes connecting it with nearby islands, the ancient mariners learned their trade.

they carried precious metals, grain, and papyrus from Egypt; tin from Asia Minor; copper from Sardinia and Cyprus; obsidian from the Aegean; and blocks of porphyry from Greece.

Transporting raw materials across long stretches of open sea required sturdy vessels. Aegean shipwrights retained the square-sail rig they might have seen on Egyptian vessels visiting Minoan ports, but they did away with the rope truss and strengthened their hulls instead by ribs fastened to a strong keel. These vessels were far better suited for work at sea, and before long the Aegean islanders were carrying not only Minoan, but also some Egyptian trade.

Unfortunately, aside from what we hear and see in contemporary Egyptian and in later Greek accounts, we know very little about the Minoan people and the ships they used. Sometime during the fifteenth century B.C., they suffered an appalling natural disaster, in which they nearly vanished from the face of the earth. With them went the ships and other clues to the maritime technology of that era. All that was left, it seemed, were a few pictures of ships carved on seals, found amid Minoan ruins on Crete. Some of the compositions were quite appealing, showing dolphins frolicking off the bow of a ship or a sea monster threatening a sailor, but they were far too small to convey much.

But there was more. During the excavations of Akrotiri, a Minoanized village on the island of Thera north of Crete, a number of extremely well preserved frescoes were found. To anyone with the slightest interest in Aegean ships, one of these in particular

The excavations in Akrotiri revealed several well-preserved frescoes, including this one, showing the first clear depictions of Aegean vessels. In time, these ships crisscrossed the eastern Mediterranean, the wine-dark sea, as Homer called it (right).

is a revelation. It shows a splendid naval parade of long and slender ships, each with a gracefully curved stem and stern, passing the waterfront. Some are propelled by rowers, others by a single square sail. The scene is one of grace and gaiety, the first to shed some light on the maritime doings of the Bronze Age Aegean.

Akrotiri owed its remarkable state of preservation to a thick layer of pumice deposited by Thera's volcano some time around 1500 B.C. As with Pompeii sixteen hundred years later, pumice sealed off the entire village, creating an instant time capsule. Many historians believe that this eruption may have triggered the end of Minoan civilization. Accompanied by earthquakes and tidal waves, the disaster could have destroyed cities and ports in one mighty sweep, leaving the island weakened and exposed. For hundreds of years wealth and power had enabled the Minoans to turn back any threat, but against this show of force they would have been defenseless.

MYCENAEAN HEROES

The demise of the Minoans and their Aegean allies enabled others to take control of the Mediterranean's sea trade. Some time after the collapse of Minos, or perhaps even before, Mycenaean Greeks began to settle in Crete, a move that allowed them to gradually take over the Minoans' extensive trading network. But others were involved in long-distance sea trading. The Canaanites, who lived along the eastern coast of the

Mediterranean, controlled the important trade routes from Mesopotamia and Central Asia, and transported eastern goods onward in their own vessels. Canaanite merchant ships have been identified on Egyptian murals, and the wreck of a Canaanite trader was found off Turkey's Cape Gelidonya, though little remained.

Cypriot, Egyptian, Syrian, and other vessels plied the Mediterranean as well, but the widespread distribution of their pottery appears to identify the Mycenaean Greeks as the principal carriers of Mediterranean trade. Unfortunately, since there is no pictorial record to speak of, we know even less about Mycenaean ships than we do about those of the Minoans and Aegean islanders. Instead, we have to rely on literature that was not much concerned with ordinary merchants and traders. It focused instead on Mycenae's heroes: the warriors who set sail for Troy during the thirteenth-century B.C.

The story of the siege, as told by Homer in the *Iliad,* and that of the long and perilous return voyage of Odysseus recounted in the *Odyssey,* sheds light on the Greeks' vessels, though Homer was writing hundreds of years after the fact. Nonetheless, he describes the ships with loving detail, comparing their gently rounded hulls to the horns of cattle. Constructed of ribs and keels, the ships were covered by jointed planks. The hulls were black, having been covered by pitch, and hollow, meaning there were no decks other than small platforms at stem and stern. Homer speaks of a fleet of twelve hundred, though that number probably became exaggerated over the years.

At times, the *Odyssey* appears to exaggerate as well. There might have been an Ithacan king named Odysseus who killed his wife's suitors upon returning from Troy, but his activities during the preceding ten years were no doubt embellished over time.

Even so, amid its description of magical places and mysterious creatures, the *Odyssey* contains much valuable nautical information. There are references to navigation, for instance, and the use of stars for night sailing. When the wrecked Odysseus is forced to build a new ship, Homer even provides us with the first known account of shipbuilding.

The task reportedly took twenty trees and a good deal of help from the goddess Calypso, who provided the tools and materials. According to Homer, Odysseus first made planks and fastened them together with mortises and tenons.

Then he "laid out the bottom" of his vessel, "set up close-set frames," and "finished up by adding the long side plankings." The hull completed, "he stepped a mast and yard, and added a broad oar to steer." Calypso, meanwhile, brought cloth for a sail; "he fashioned that too, a fine one." After completing the rigging, Homer continued, Odysseus put the craft on rollers and "hauled it down to the sea."

Homer observed this technique as it was applied during the seventh century B.C., more than five hundred years later. But the discovery of a thirty-five-hundred-year-old merchant ship wrecked off the Turkish coast at Ulu Burun proved that Bronze Age shipwrights were building ships the same way. The excavation team found a few sections of the hull buried under the sand. Its planks were fastened to the keel and to one another by mortises and tenons pinned by hardwood pegs, indicating that little had changed in shipbuilding techniques between the time of its construction and Homer's era.

The wreck also revealed a treasure trove of cargo from all corners of the ancient Mediterranean: copper ingots and pottery from Cyprus; tin from Turkey; Canaanite glass, jewelry and amphorae; Mycenaean pottery; ebony-like wood from Nubia in sub-tropical Africa; ivory from Syria; cylinder seals from Mesopotamia; and tools and weapons from Egypt. To obtain such a wide variety of wares, the ship probably sailed a circular route, from the easternmost Mediterranean to Cyprus, Rhodes, and the Aegean; then south to Crete and North Africa, and back east via Egypt. The lavish cargo also suggests that the vessel may have been on a special mission, perhaps carrying a royal consignment from one ruler to another.

Little is known about the ship's nationality. George Bass, director of the Institute of Nautical Archaeology at Texas A&M University, suspects it was Mycenaean or Canaanite, or perhaps Cypriote. But since there are so few pictures of ships of that period to cross-reference, its precise origin may never be known. Even so, the wreck has shed a great deal of light on Bronze Age Mediterranean shipping, revealing that sturdy, well-built ships maintained regular trade links throughout much of the area.

Sometime around 1200 B.C., the established ways and patterns were disrupted by major demographic changes. Mycenaean civilization abruptly ended, as northern invaders overran the country. Rebellious border tribes overthrew the Hittite empire, which controlled much of Asia Minor and the eastern Mediterranean. Cyprus was invaded and destroyed, as was the Syrian coast. Only Egypt managed to repel the invaders, though it would not be much longer before the New Kingdom's influence began to wane and the established order there collapsed as well.

Much of this upheaval has been attributed to the Sea Peoples—a collective term for bands of raiders who probably came from Asia Minor. Not much is known about these people, aside from what was left by the Egyptians, who defeated them on two occasions. The Great Temple of Ramses III, who ruled Egypt at the time, contains unique reliefs of the battles, showing ships locked in a fierce fight near the mouth of the Nile. The pictures make clear that the invaders were routed: their boats were capsized and their crews systematically massacred by Egyptian archers positioned on boats as

well as on shore. Inscriptions complement the scene of devastation: "they were grappled, capsized and laid out on the shore dead, their ships made heaps from stem to stern."

How much of this is to be taken literally is difficult to say. Ramses' biographers were not modest, repeatedly praising the pharaoh's strategic and organizational skills and speaking of troops so well prepared that they "were like lions roaring on the mountain top." But the reliefs show much that is new, including the only depiction of the Sea Peoples' ships. They appear to be somewhat smaller than the Egyptian vessels, though they have the same rig, deck, superstructure, and crow's nest. Their hulls are different, however, with raised stems and sterns adorned with the heads of birds. Unlike the Egyptian ships, the vessels shown in these reliefs have no rowers, presumably because they were doubling as fighters. The ships' lack of maneuverability put them at the mercy of the Egyptians, who clearly did not waste the opportunity.

GREECE AND THE SEA

Similar ships seem to have existed along the Mediterranean's easternmost coast—in Syria and Canaan. In time a new generation of seafarers arose in this region: the Phoenicians. From strategically located ports their mariners fanned all over the eastern Mediterranean in sturdy, well-manned ships, dominating much of its trade for half a millennium (see Chapter 2).

Trade in the eastern Mediterranean declined during the upheaval created by the Sea Peoples. Cyprus too was invaded and destroyed.

By the ninth century B.C., the great population movements that affected so much of the region began to subside. Gradually a more settled way of life returned, and with it trade increased. At first the Phoenicians continued to dominate sea trade, but, as they ventured further west, they inevitably lost some of their control. A number of competitors stepped in, eager to claim their share, though none more determined than the people who had invaded Greece a few hundred years earlier. By the eighth century they had formed an alliance of independent city-states that was strong enough to begin demanding a major role in the affairs of the ancient world.

During the next hundred years or so, the Greeks established trading posts along the coasts of the Mediterranean to gain a greater share of its growing trade, the same way the Phoenicians had done along the coast of North Africa and Spain. But their settlements did not remain isolated pockets of traders and businessmen; they expanded and before long became full-fledged colonies. By the sixth century B.C., no less than 250 of them dotted the shores of the Black Sea and the Mediterranean. A healthy trade developed between the various colonies, contributing in no small part to the development of a well-organized merchant fleet.

Greek trade routes penetrated deep into the wheat-producing regions of the Black Sea, and south and west into the Mediterranean, and they handled goods ranging from oriental luxuries to raw materials. Competition with the Phoenicians ensued, and frequent clashes occurred. The most serious came in 480 B.C. at Salamis, where a Phoenician contingent sided with a strong Persian fleet. Against strong odds the Greeks prevailed, thereby strengthening their political and commercial position in the region.

With the rise of Greek civilization, the picture of ancient Western seafaring brightens considerably. The Greeks not only documented their maritime activities, they also often depicted them.

With the Greeks' emergence as the dominant power of antiquity, our picture of Western shipping brightens considerably. No longer do we have to resort to speculation caused by lack of evidence, as was the case with the Minoans, Mycenaeans, the Sea Peoples, and even the secretive Phoenicians. The Greeks simply made a point of describing and visually documenting their maritime achievements. Compared to what their competitors left, the Greeks' depictions of ships—on pottery, plates, walls, and tombs—are a revelation. Combined with the reports of historians and travelers, these representations create a vibrant picture of the world of shipping in ancient times.

Even so, there are a few shortcomings. Pottery artists usually knew little about ships or seafaring, and their ships occasionally look awkward. Given a choice, they also preferred to depict fancy galleys rather than plump cargo carriers, leaving relatively few pictures of merchant ships. Literature similarly favored tales of heroic naval deeds over everyday trading voyages, giving us the impression that far more galleys filled with heroes crisscrossed the Aegean than did ordinary merchant ships.

We know, of course, that this was not the case. Then, as now, merchant ships predominated because they were by far the most efficient mode of transportation. But the ancient Greeks recorded few of their everyday maritime doings expressly for posterity. What we know has been gathered mostly from chance finds like a merchant's ledger or, as in the case of Bronze Age seaborne trade, from ships that never reached their destination.

Andreas Cariolou, a sponge diver from Kyrenia in Cyprus, found one such wreck in 1965. When a team of American archaeologists arrived in Cyprus not long thereafter, Cariolou told them of his find and guided them to the site. The first few dives showed the wreck to be a major find. Though only a small pile of amphorae was visible, it appeared that much of the cargo was buried beneath. More importantly, there were good indications that much of the hull was preserved as well.

Several years of meticulous excavation confirmed this assessment. The "Kyrenia ship," as it soon became known, was a Greek coastal trader, about fifty feet long, which went down during the fourth century B.C. Though more than a thousand years younger than the Ulu Burun ship, it was constructed in the same way: first a keel was laid; then the outer strakes, joined edge to edge by mortises and tenons, were built up; and into this shell frames were inserted to support the hull. Radioactive dating of the timbers and coins found at the site revealed that the vessel was at least eighty years old when it sank, a notable lifespan for a small wooden trader.

What makes the Kyrenia ship so valuable is that it was simply an ordinary ship, on a run from Rhodes with a cargo of wine and almonds. Unlike the information from pottery and literature, the Kyrenia wreck revealed how the Greeks built their vessels in the fourth century B.C., what materials they used, where they traded, and what they carried. Nothing was left of the rigging or the crew, but four identical sets of utensils—drinking cups, plates, spoons and oil jugs—suggest something about the number of people aboard. Their fate is unknown. Perhaps pirates attacked the ship; more likely a sudden storm overtook her. The absence of personal belongings suggests that the crew may even have had a chance to get away.

ROMAN SEA TRADE

By the time the Kyrenia ship sank, Greece's domination of the ancient trade routes had begun to decline. Gradually, the trade of the eastern Mediterranean became more evenly divided among a number of other states. Some were small, independent states like Rhodes, which depended almost entirely on sea trade. They competed against the major powers of the area, Egypt and Macedonia, which had maritime ambitions of their own. The western Mediterranean, in contrast, was dominated by the powerful Carthaginians. The heirs to Phoenicia's maritime legacy, they operated from Carthage in northern Africa.

Piraeus has been Athens' provisioning port for more than 2,500 years. The small Kyrenia ship probably visited the harbor several times during its 80-year lifespan.

During the third century B.C., a new power emerged. A society of soldiers, farmers, and merchants, Rome did not show much maritime ambition at first. But as the empire gradually expanded, its citizens were forced to turn to the sea. Troops and supplies had to be carried to all corners of the empire, and a maritime presence became indispensable.

It did not take long for this growing presence to run counter to Carthaginian interests, and for a hundred years the two nations were locked in a fierce struggle for maritime supremacy. When Rome emerged victorious in the mid-second-century B.C., it found itself in control of the Mediterranean. Until the division of the Empire some five hundred years later, Rome would be the greatest maritime power the world had ever known, almost in spite of itself.

One would not expect great nautical advances from a nation of landlubbers, and Rome was no exception. The design of its merchant vessels was based on Greek carriers,

A third-century marble relief shows a rescue operation in the harbor at Portus, successor to Ostia. The vessel on the right has the small bowsprit sail the Romans added to their ships.

and Roman fighting ships adopted many characteristics from their Carthaginian opponents. But the Romans would not have reached their position by merely imitating others. Occasionally they added something of their own: a small bowsprit sail known as the *artemon*, for instance, which was placed on their larger merchant carriers to help their maneuverability. Roman galleys were also equipped with a novelty: the *corvus*, a spiked gangway that could be dropped onto enemy vessels to help convert a sea battle into an infantry battle across decks. But most importantly, the Romans elevated maritime commerce onto an entirely new level. By the first century A.D., Roman colonies surrounded the entire Mediterranean, and the trade flowing between the colonies and into the Imperial City demanded an entirely new maritime infrastructure.

As with the Greeks, the Romans' seaborne trade is well documented. Numerous frescoes, stone reliefs, and mosaics depict Rome's maritime doings. Vivid accounts from writers and historians like Pliny the Elder, Ovid, Strabo, and Lucian back up this pictorial account. The discovery of several sunken ships has further aided our understanding of Roman seafaring. Many wrecks were looted before archaeologists ever got to them, but a sufficient number could be properly excavated. This work confirmed that the Romans continued building their ships along patterns established much earlier, that is, with the planks attached to one another with mortises and tenons.

The excavations also revealed the impressive nature of Roman vessels. Surveys of some remaining hull sections, for instance, indicated that they belonged to ships measuring more than two hundred tons. Judging from their cargoes, these vessels were sent east to carry marble building materials. Even larger ships were used to carry grain from Egypt. Lucian described one of these as being one hundred and eighty feet long, forty-five feet wide, and forty-four feet deep from deck to keel. Awed by her size and a crew "as large as an army," the Greek historian repeated the crew's claim that "she could carry enough grain to satisfy every mouth in Athens for a full year." Whether or not this was true, these ships could obviously carry a vast amount of grain—perhaps as much as a thousand tons.

Ships like this, or even smaller ones, could not proceed up the Tiber to Rome. For this reason the Romans constructed a large port at Ostia, near the river's mouth, where inbound cargoes could be loaded onto barges for the trip to the capital. By the first century A.D., astounding amounts of goods passed along Ostia's wharves. The importation of grain from North Africa alone, for instance, totaled more than one hundred and fifty tons per year. Massive amounts of marble and other building materials from Greece, Egypt, and Asia Minor—needed for Rome's many construction projects—passed across the wharves as well. And always there were ships from other corners of the empire, carrying silks from China, spices from India and Southeast Asia, cosmetics and fragrances from Arabia, and wine from Spain and the Greek islands.

During its heyday in the first and second century Ostia was undoubtedly one of the busiest places in the Roman Empire. But towards the end of that period the port began to silt up, and much of its traffic moved to the harbor of Portus northwest of the city. A gradual decline set in and, though Ostia managed to retain some commercial activity, the city never recaptured its position as the empire's principal port.

The fall of the Western Roman Empire early in the fifth century brought the end of Ostia as a functional port. For the next two hundred years, the city suffered from multiple invasions that caused much destruction and a massive population drain. Thereafter, Ostia became a quarry of sorts, where Romans, Genoans, and Pisans came to fetch building materials. The plunder lasted until well into the eighteenth century, when the remaining ruins were thoroughly combed for sculptures and other art objects.

During the nineteenth century the looting finally halted, and Ostia underwent the first of a series of excavations, designed to reach the city's street level of the early second century A.D. In spite of the enormous destruction that had occurred over the previous fifteen hundred years, a remarkable city was uncovered, with nineteen public baths, twenty-two villas, one hundred and sixty-two apartment buildings, several temples, one theater, and a number of stores.

Although the Tiber had long before changed its course, many of the ruins were reminders that Ostia had been a major port. There were huge warehouses, for instance, and the remains of wharves. Behind the theater was the *Piazza delle Corporazioni*—a large square that once held the offices of more than seventy companies. Most of them had maritime ties, as the mosaic pavements in front indicate. Like Rome's Forum, Ostia's remains now are no more than silent witnesses to a long-ago past, but they, perhaps better than anything else, reflect the vast scale of the empire's maritime commerce.

The remnants of Ostia, once the largest port in the Roman Empire. The mosaic pavements in the Piazza delle Corporazioni escaped centuries of looting and plunder, providing a splendid picture of the many types of ships that once called here.

NORTHERN DEVELOPMENTS

With the incursions of Goths, Vandals, and others invaders, the maritime focus of the Mediterranean shifted east again. Ruled from Constantinople, the Eastern Roman Empire was more successful in repelling the so-called barbarians, but it no longer played a pioneering role in the story of seafaring. The wreck of a seventh-century Byzantine trader that was excavated near Yassi Ada in Turkey proved a veritable time capsule, but it did not reveal major changes when compared to the ships that traded in the area hundreds of years earlier.

Later ships did not advance a great deal either. Ninth-century Greek manuscripts include some paintings of Byzantine vessels that show them to be small traders with rounded hulls and two steering oars. They appear similar to their counterparts of classical times, with the exception of their lateen sails. But these sails can hardly be called a Western invention, having been introduced when a growing number of Arab ships began appearing in the eastern Mediterranean during the late seventh century.

In northern and western Europe, ships underwent greater changes. Though the Romans had controlled part of this region, their presence does not appear to have had a great effect on local shipbuilding traditions. Instead, shipwrights kept to their own methods, building ships that relied on nails or stitching rather than mortises and tenons. Among the several excavated boats from this era, a few were built along

Mediterranean lines, with hull planks tenoned and the frames inserted afterwards, but perhaps these were built and used by the Romans themselves, while the locals kept mostly to their own craft.

The Romans described some of these indigenous ships. Caesar, for instance, wrote about the boats and rafts encountered during his northern campaigns. In his *De Bello Gallico (The Gallic Wars)* he meticulously described the seagoing ships of the Veneti, a tribe that lived along the northwestern French coast. They were broad ships with high bows and sterns, and a single square sail. Well suited for rough waters, they probably were among the most advanced ships built in northern Europe at that time.

Caesar had good reasons for his keen observations because the Veneti tribe's vessels proved more than a match for his own. In their final confrontation the Romans only secured victory after they managed to cut the shrouds of their enemy's ships, rendering them immobile. That enabled Roman soldiers to board the enemy vessels and convert the engagement into a battle across decks—a skill they mastered better than anyone else.

Further north, there were no Romans and hence no written records about ships or anything else for several more centuries. Rock carvings show us what kinds of craft people were using in these areas, but the archaeological record is far more helpful. Some finds indicate that people still relied on dugout canoes and skin boats, as their ancestors had since time immemorial. But others reveal some of the northern shipwrights' innovations. To make dugouts more seaworthy, for instance, they added a few strakes along their sides to provide a higher freeboard. Then, rather than joining the side planks edge to edge, they made them overlap slightly, and sewed them together or hammered them onto inserted frames. Finally they raised bow and stern, enabling the boats to handle rougher waters.

No one knows the exact origin of these particular practices, but the type of craft that resulted was the forerunner of what would become one of the most feared ships of all time.

In the late eighth century the inhabitants of England and Ireland caught their first glimpse of these ships. It was a sight few would forget, if they lived to tell the tale. Wherever they went, Viking ships brought terror and destruction. Men, women, and children were massacred, their villages plundered and burned. The Vikings looted cities and towns, even as far inland as Paris. The chronicles of western Europe began to report tales of unimaginable suffering. *A furore Normannorum libera nos*, people prayed—from the fury of the Norsemen deliver us. But their prayer was not heard. For two centuries the Norsemen plundered their way into western Europe. They came from the sea and vanished into it, if they left at all.

The Vikings were a Scandinavian people, living in what are now Norway, Sweden, and Denmark. What caused them to turn from peaceful traders to brutal invaders in the course of barely a century remains unclear. Presumably the weather played a role, with rising temperatures improving conditions in northern Europe, thereby allowing more people to survive. The population may have grown too rapidly to be peacefully absorbed, forcing people to leave. Some went overland or across the Baltic, but during the seventh century the Vikings developed a ship that could handle long sea voyages. Not long thereafter they set out on their murderous raids, first across the North Sea to Ireland, Scotland, and England, and later to the coasts of France and the Low Countries.

The Vikings' longboat was not just a capable ship, it was one of the best ships made anywhere in Europe at the time. Like its predecessors, it was built in shell sequence,

with the hull planks overlapping one another. But unlike earlier craft, the longboat had a pronounced keel to provide directional stability. During the seventh century the Vikings also added a mast with a broad, rectangular sail. It transformed their boats from coastal craft to seaworthy ships.

The Vikings treated these vessels with care bordering on reverence. They gave them brave or even poetic names like *Lion of the Waves*, *Raven of the Wind*, and *Long Serpent*—the latter of which, at a reported one hundred and fifty feet, was the most famous Viking ship of all. To a warrior these ships symbolized manhood, adventure, respect, and wealth. In fact, no greater honor could befall a Viking than to die in battle and be buried along with his ship.

Some of these burial ships were found in superb condition, even after more than a thousand years under the ground. Though short of a blueprint, they have enabled maritime historians to determine that Viking shipwrights selected only the finest timbers and carved the planks by axe along the grain of the wood, so that they would retain maximum strength and flexibility. After the keel and posts were laid, the planks were placed from one end to the other, producing a strong and resilient hull about one hundred feet in length. Then ribs and crossbeams were inserted to provide lateral strength, and the hull was caulked with twisted and tarred animal hairs to make it watertight.

Usually there were only sixteen planks on either side, keeping the ship light and flexible enough to ride atop the waves rather than plow through them. This allowed longboats to skim across the water, easily reaching speeds of ten knots and more in

Not all of the Vikings' vessels were used for their notorious raids. Meticulously constructed replicas of the ships found in Roskilde Fjord make clear their ships were built for a variety of purposes. Whatever their function, they were all extremely well built. A burial ship like the one found in Oseberg (right) also sported exquisite carvings.

favorable winds. With a yard that could be braced around the mast, the ships could even sail into the wind, held onto their course by their keel and a steering oar on the quarter.

Fast ships do not necessarily make for comfortable sailing, and Viking longboats were no exception. To keep the vessels light, their builders used only a few components. Aside from keel, stem, stern, strakes, and ribs, there might have been deck planks and rowing benches, but little to protect anyone against the elements. Viking seafarers often encountered bad weather in northern seas, and conditions aboard must have been appalling. Their sagas describe these hardships, speaking of long voyages in cold and unknown seas. There is a somber undercurrent to them, though never a complaint. They were far too tough a breed for that.

As is the case with most accounts of heroic deeds, the Vikings' sagas are short on more modest endeavors such as trading. It is unfortunate because the Vikings were traders long before they became raiders, and they continued to trade throughout much of the Viking era. Occasionally they used longboats for coastal commerce, but their merchants relied mostly on short, beamy vessels called *knarrs*. Of course, no Viking chieftain wanted to be buried in something as mundane as a trading ship, so our knowledge of these ships was very limited until the discovery of several sunken *knarrs* at the entrance of Roskilde Fjord in Denmark. Remarkably well preserved, the ships turned out to be built in the same manner as the swifter longboats but with heavier planking and a deeper keel.

Though perhaps best known for terrorizing much of western and northern Europe, the Vikings had a highly developed sense of law and order that probably accounted for their great voyages into the Atlantic. The standard punishment for many crimes was banishment, and it was that bleak prospect that caused a number of Danish and Norwegian Vikings to pack their belongings onto a ship and seek a new life to the west. By the ninth century they had reached the Faeroe Islands and Iceland, and a century later they landed in Greenland. They colonized all these areas—even Greenland, where two settlements were founded in the late tenth century.

There is no doubt that Vikings from these colonies reached North America. Early in the eleventh century, they even made an effort to settle a colony in Vinland— today's Newfoundland. But life there proved too difficult. After three years of constant harassment by natives, the settlers left and returned to Greenland.

Though worsening climatic conditions did not allow them to maintain a permanent presence in Greenland either, this western expansion was one of the Vikings' greatest achievements. Five hundred years before any of the great explorers, Viking sailors crossed the North Atlantic several times, without the benefit of maps or navigational instruments. Their sagas demonstrate their knowledge of navigating by the sun and the stars; mostly, however, the Vikings relied on their innate understanding of the sea, following natural clues like clouds and currents, the flight path of birds, or even the color of the water.

Around the same time, Swedish Vikings ventured east, using their shallow draft vessels to sail up Russia's rivers into the country's heartland. After establishing settlements at Novgorod and Smolensk, they continued south, using the Dnieper River to reach Kiev and the Black Sea. At first they clashed with the Slavic peoples encountered along the way, but eventually the Vikings settled these regions and focused on trade, realizing that they could tap into important North-South trade routes. Before long, their traders shuttled back and forth, carrying commodities like furs and dried fish south, and returning with oriental luxuries obtained from Muslim traders. Some of them made a fortune, proving that long-term commercial relations were far more profitable than the hit-and-run raids of their past.

MEDIEVAL VESSEL TYPES

Eventually the Vikings settled in many other regions, from East Anglia to Normandy and even as far south as Sicily. Contrary to their reputation, the settlers turned out to be efficient administrators, who introduced new laws and a centralized form of government. In the process they changed the political and economic landscape, paving the way for Europe's transition to feudalism and the Middle Ages.

Relative peace returned to the region. After centuries of languishing under a stagnant economy, Europeans saw signs of a recovery, based in large part on vastly improved farming techniques. Increased productivity not only permitted more people to be fed, it also freed up time for them to do other things. Many farmers left their fields and turned to trades in nearby villages, including weaving, tanning, and masonry. The villages grew; some even became small towns.

At first these specialized tradesmen geared their work to meet local needs, but as their numbers grew so did their output, creating a surplus. Before long different regions began to export particular goods. Italy made fine linens; the Baltic had fish; and Germany produced beer, copper, and silver. France exported wines; England, tin and wool; Spain specialized in exquisite leatherwork; and Flanders in textiles. To handle this vast increase in trade, merchants needed an efficient trading network, in which ships played a vital role.

For some time merchants relied on larger versions of the double-ended Viking ship, though they decked them over to protect the cargo. But during the late twelfth century the stern rudder made its appearance in the West, bringing about some changes. Stern rudders did not fit round-hulled ships very well, so shipwrights began to build ships with straight sterns. They also installed keel planks and flat bottoms, which allowed the ships to ground on a sandy bottom. The result was a very different type of ship, known as a cog.

In comparison to their Viking counterparts, cogs were slow and bulky but they could carry up to ten times as much cargo. Having to plow through the sea and possessing no ability to make headway into the wind, they did not sail as well, but they were reliable. Cogs even proved to be relatively safe because their high sides made boarding by pirates more difficult. No other vessel type combined these qualities, and for several hundred years cogs dominated northern Europe's sea trade, carrying wool from England, cloth from Flanders, salt and wine from France, timber and grain from Germany, iron and copper from Norway, and salted herring from the Baltic.

As trade volumes continued to grow, so did the size of ships. During the fourteenth century, a new ship type called a hulk replaced the cog. Like the cog, it had only one sail and was built in shell sequence, with the hull planks overlapping one another. But with it, clinker-built ships began to reach their maximum size. To build even larger ships, northern shipwrights turned to Mediterranean construction techniques, where ships

The first depictions of stern rudders on Western vessels have been found on Flemish reliefs, including this one, seen on the baptismal font of the church of Zedelgem (Belgium). Winchester Cathedral possesses a Flemish font as well, with a similar theme.

were carvel-built, with the planks laid edge to edge. Used with pre-constructed frames, this method supported much larger hulls, and gradually northern cargo ships abandoned their clinker-built (overlapping) hulls for smooth carvel-built sides.

Larger ships needed more sail to drive them forward, so first a second mast was added, and later a third or even a fourth. Northern shipbuilders kept to square sails on the foremast and mainmasts, but rigged a small lateen sail, also adopted from the Mediterranean, on the third or mizzenmast. Thus the merging of two shipbuilding traditions began to result in a new type of ship: the West's multi-masted sailing vessel.

The first ship to emerge from this marriage between northern and southern shipbuilding traditions was the carrack, a bulky cargo carrier that soon became a common sight all over Europe. Its three masts not only provided greater forward motion, they also enabled the vessel to sail closer to the wind, with the lateen-rigged mizzenmast helping to counter the windage caused by a high forecastle. Though by no means a great sailing ship, the carrack represented a revolution. With it Europe finally had a vessel that could do more than just carry large cargoes. Unlike its predecessors, it could sail just about anywhere, even in less favorable winds, and safely return.

THE AGE OF EXPLORATION

Carracks and other three-masted ships appeared at a time when Europe was ready to use them to the fullest. Trade volumes kept growing year after year, keeping larger ships

busy. But there was also a rapidly growing demand for oriental goods like silks and especially spices—pepper, cloves, nutmeg, and cinnamon—that made northern Europe's drab diets somewhat more palatable.

This lucrative trade was largely in the hands of the Arabs. Their dhows regularly sailed to India and China, returning to their Persian Gulf ports with eastern luxuries. From there the goods were carried overland to the Mediterranean, where they were transshipped for the final leg to Western markets. Immense fortunes were made in this trade, and European nations wanted to claim what they considered their rightful share. But to do so they had to bypass the Arabs. The only way to accomplish this was by sea.

In this setting Portugal's Henry the Navigator began to send vessels south along the African coast early in the fifteenth century, hoping to find an all-water route to Africa's gold. At first Henry's sailors used small single-masted vessels that slowly progressed along the northwest African coast. But once past the Canary Islands, the crews invariably hesitated. There, so the reasoning went, was the Green Sea of Darkness—a region where the sun passed so close to the sea that it hissed and steamed. Tradition held that it was impassable.

Sailors who ventured as far as Cape Non returned with tales of adverse winds and frightening currents. They also claimed to have discerned a region of perpetual fog further south, from which there was no return. As if to prove the point, two Genoese ships that ventured that way never returned. Although their ill-fated voyage had taken place more than a hundred years earlier, most sailors were aware of it.

During the excavation of a new dock in the port of Antwerp in late 2000, a rare 14th-century cog was discovered. The missing section of the hull was ripped out by a crane.

To Henry's credit, he compelled his mariners to disregard these rumors, and gradually make their way further south. After thirteen or fourteen voyages they neared Cape Bojador, a place barely noticeable on a map, but then believed to be an impassable barrier. It was an uninviting place, marked by shallows, strong winds, and persistent currents, but it was far more than a mere physical barrier. Medieval scribes described it as the end of the world: a place that led straight to the fires of hell. No wonder none of Henry's mariners volunteered to be the first to round it.

Henry commissioned Gil Eanes, one of his most capable mariners, to pass Bojador. It took Eanes two tries. The first time he got within sight of the Cape, but was forced to return when his crew refused to go on. The second time he gave it a wide berth, headed to sea, and sailed on. A few days later he set a course east again, and landed in a small bay, about a hundred miles south of the feared cape. For a place that was supposed to mark the end of the world, it was remarkably calm and unmemorable. Even the currents that were supposed to prevent his return were running gently along the shore.

The caravel became the preferred vessel of exploration of Portuguese mariners. Its task consisted of collecting geographic information, not necessarily large cargoes.

With the rounding of Bojador in 1434, Eanes crossed the barrier between myth and reality, allowing the business of exploration to begin in earnest. But first there was a need for a better ship. Henry's mariners felt that their squared-rigged vessels did not make sufficient progress against the prevailing headwinds on the homeward voyage, so Portuguese shipwrights designed a new type of vessel. Called a caravel, it was lateen-rigged to improve its ability to head into the wind, and shallow-drafted to approach unknown shores. The end result was a ship that was small and versatile enough to sail just about anywhere.

Portuguese caravels were soon making rapid progress along the African coast. Between 1444 and 1446 no less than thirty voyages were dispatched, culminating with Dinis Dias's rounding of Cape Verde, Africa's westernmost point. In 1455, Alvise da Cadamosto, a Venetian sailing for Portugal, reached the Gambia River. By the time of Henry's death in 1460, his mariners had reached Sierra Leone. It was only one-third of the way down the African coast, but nobody knew that.

After a ten-year interruption, the voyages continued. From Lisbon, caravels left regularly for the African coast, constantly pushing back the borders of the unknown. Along the way, the Portuguese established trading stations. They gathered gold and slaves from the African interior and sent them to Portugal, generating revenues that allowed the expensive business of exploration to continue.

By the 1470s the Portuguese had expanded their sights beyond Africa to the Indies. This new objective required a sea passage between the Atlantic and Indian Oceans. No one knew how far it was, or whether it even existed, but they continued. In 1473 Lopo Gonçalves crossed the equator. By 1486 Diogo Cão had reached Cape Cross, in what is now Namibia. And just two years later Bartolomeu Dias sailed the final thousand miles to the southern tip of Africa. Encountering rough weather, he called it the Cape of Storms, but the Portuguese king renamed it the Cape of Good Hope—Good Hope, for now the way to the Indies was finally open.

Ten years later, on May 18, 1498, Vasco da Gama attained the long-sought objective, reaching India's Malabar Coast after a brutal ten-month voyage. He took four ships, including two armed *naos*. Designed specifically for the expedition, they were large, three-masted vessels with a topsail on the mainmast and plenty of room for a

THE LONGITUDE PUZZLE SOLVED

On October 29, 1628, the *Batavia,* the Dutch East Indies Company's newest retour ship, set out on her maiden voyage, bound for the Cape and the East Indies. None of the 300 crew and passengers aboard knew that they had booked a one-way trip to tragedy.

The voyage started out well enough. After calling at the Dutch settlement of Cape Town, the *Batavia* headed south towards the roaring forties. The ship made good time before the strong westerlies, much better than anyone had anticipated. Captain Pelsaert expected to be turning north towards the Indonesian island of Java before long, but figured he should take advantage of the steady winds a few more days. He was wrong. Early in the morning of June 4, 1629, under perfectly clear skies, his ship ran aground on the Abrolhos Islands, some fifty miles west of the Australian mainland. No one, least of all Pelsaert, realized that the ship had already come so far.

Virtually everyone aboard survived the grounding, but the *Batavia* was a loss. Pelsaert accordingly divided the sailors, passengers, and soldiers among the various islands, and set out with a skeleton crew in one of the ship's boats to find water and perhaps a more hospitable area. But there was nothing to be found on the Australian mainland; "an accursed land," Pelsaert called it. He continued to Batavia, hoping to return with help in time.

Against heavy odds Pelsaert reached Batavia, but by the time he returned to the Abrolhos Islands three months later, no less than 125 people had been massacred by a small group of mutineers. Many more had succumbed to disease and malnutrition. After the mutineers were hung, only seventy-four of the original 300 reached their final destination.

The *Batavia's* unfortunate maiden voyage entered nautical lore, and for much of the seventeenth century the story was told and retold in Holland and the rest of Europe. But what happened to the ship was not uncommon at that time. Many ships wrecked on known or unknown reefs for the simple reason that their captains and navigators, when out of sight of land, never knew exactly where they were. They knew how to calculate their latitude, using the sun or stars, but longitude had to be estimated on the basis of dead reckoning: a combination of speed, winds, currents, leeway, experience, and whatever else was thought to influence a ship's progress.

Errors caused by dead reckoning increased with the amount of time a ship was out in the open sea; in the Pacific, where voyages out of sight of land of several weeks and more were common, they multiplied in size. Nothing could be done about this until the key to longitude could be discovered.

Actually, finding the key was not so difficult; it had already been defined in 1474 when a German astronomer pointed out that longitude required accurate timekeeping. Since the earth rotates 360 degrees in twenty-four hours, or fifteen degrees per hour, any mariner who knew the exact times at his current location and his place of departure could determine how far east or west he had traveled. All he had to do was to multiply the time difference by fifteen.

Of course, that was easier said than done. Finding local time was relatively easy; a determination of the sun's highest position in the sky indicated local noon. But a clock that could tell what time it was elsewhere at that very moment was out of the question. Hourglasses were very unreliable, leading to errors of hundreds of miles. Even spring-driven clocks were useless; temperature differences caused their metals to expand and contract, making their readings inaccurate. That left only dead reckoning. Sometimes it was remarkably accurate, but much of the time it was not, as Pelsaert and countless others found out.

In the early eighteenth century, after yet another brutal wreck was blamed on an inaccurate position fix, the British Parliament decided to try to solve the problem for once and for all, promising a reward of 20,000 pounds for any "generally practical and useful method" of finding longitude at sea within thirty miles after a six-week voyage. Twenty thousand pounds was a stupendous amount of money at that time; it would have kept anyone stylishly set up for life. Other nations had also offered rewards, but this was by far the largest and hence the most interesting. To promote a variety of solutions, lower amounts were offered for less precise methods: 15,000 pounds for errors of less than forty miles and 10,000 pounds for errors not exceeding sixty miles.

To supervise the competition, Parliament appointed a Board of Longitude. One of its members was Isaac Newton, who explained that various methods existed, all of which were "difficult to execute." First on his list, however, was the watch "to keep time exactly." But, as he added, "by reason of the Motion of a Ship, the Variation of Heat and Cold, Wet and Dry, and the Difference of Gravity in different latitudes, such a Watch Hath not yet been made." He thought it unlikely that it ever would be.

Newton also mentioned methods using astronomical observations, including one that depended on the position of the moon in relation to the sun and the stars. It relied on the fact that, if the motion of the moon is known, it is possible to derive tables forecasting its angular momentum from the sun and certain fixed stars as observed on a standard meridian. In 1752 Tobias Mayer, a German astronomer, actually succeeded

John Harrison's first timekeeper, also known as Harrison I. A bit too bulky to take along on a ship, but it still runs precisely.

in compiling these tables, but the method he came up with was so complex that it took several hours of calculations to get one fix. Two of the greatest Pacific navigators, James Cook and his French counterpart Louis Antoine de Bougainville, relied on Mayer's system to determine their positions at sea, often to within one degree. But Cook and de Bougainville were on surveying missions, and their skill and determination could hardly be expected on a simple merchant carrier. The Board of Longitude accordingly rejected Mayer's method. Accurate it was, but "generally practicable and useful" was another matter.

That left only the Watch, and it took an extraordinary man to finally construct it. He was John Harrison, a Yorkshire carpenter turned clockmaker, who took on the problem as his life's mission in 1714, and devoted the next fifty years to constructing not one, but four clocks that met the board's requirements. The key to his achievement was a pendulum composed of brass and steel: two metals that expand and contract at different rates and thus allow for a near-constant period, unaffected by temperature changes. Harrison also developed an escapement that never required oiling, and with these two original inventions he proceeded to construct the most accurate clocks ever built, unaffected by "the Motion of a Ship, the Variation of Heat and Cold and Wet and Dry" and all the other factors Newton had summed up. Of his fourth watch,

a veritable timekeeping masterpiece, he exclaimed, "I think I may make bold to say there is neither any Mechanical or Mathematical thing in the World that is more beautiful or curious in texture than this, my watch or Timekeeper."

That, of course, was a highly personal opinion, but Harrison was not far from the truth. The marine watch, or chronometer as it became known, was the West's single most important contribution to the science of navigation. China invented the compass, and the Arabs contributed astronomy and mathematics—all of which were developed by generations of scientists and mariners. The West's marine chronometer, in contrast, was the achievement of a single man.

Though Harrison's chronometers were tested in 1764 and exceeded the reward conditions laid down by the Board of Longitude, it took another ten years before he was finally paid. By then John Harrison was eighty years old. Three years later he died. Perhaps James Cook paid Harrison's achievements the greatest tribute when he readily switched his lunar tables for a copy of Harrison's fourth chronometer on subsequent voyages. Soon Cook referred to it as "our trusted friend, the Watch" and "our never-failing guide."

cargo of spices. One of these and a smaller caravel returned the following year after a twenty-seven-thousand-mile voyage. Da Gama and his surviving companions received a tumultuous welcome in Lisbon. Though they returned with no more than a handful of spices, what was stowed in the hold was less important than what could be fit in the mind of a man: the information necessary to secure the sea route to the Indies and its riches.

Within a year, Portugal had another expedition on its way east, this time a massive fleet of thirteen armed cargo ships under the command of Pedro Álvares Cabral. Following Da Gama's example, Cabral led his fleet wide to the west of Africa to take advantage of the trade winds. But he went too far and landed in Brazil, which he claimed for Portugal before pressing on. Despite the detour and atrocious weather near the Cape, he reached Calicut after a six-month voyage. Seven of his ships eventually returned to Lisbon, heavily laden with spices.

Already a new expedition was ready to sail, and from then on Portugal sent out annual fleets. Before long, Lisbon became Europe's spice market, much to the dismay of the Venetians who had controlled the western end of this lucrative trade until then.

While Portugal went south and east on its way to the Indies, Spain tried to get there by going west, an option defended with near-missionary zeal by Christopher Columbus. Trained in Portugal, Columbus expected to reach the Far East after a thirty-five-hundred-mile crossing of the Atlantic—nearly nine thousand miles less than the real distance. Fortunately for him, the vast American landmass stood in the way. But Columbus stood by his original calculations and, for the remainder of his life, was convinced he had reached the East by sailing west.

Like his Portuguese counterparts, Columbus relied on a couple of caravels to make his historic crossing. The smallest was lateen-rigged; the other square-rigged. There was also a larger vessel, the *Santa Maria*—much bulkier and slower than the others. Though the *Santa Maria* served as his flagship, Columbus never referred to her other than as "the ship." Unimpressed with her abilities, he called her "unfit for discovery." Columbus may even have been relieved when she was lost off Haiti, so he did not have to take her back against the prevailing easterlies.

Even so, the *Santa Maria* represented the type of vessel that would soon be sailing regularly across the Atlantic to the New World. Like Da Gama's *naos*, this type of larger vessel made it possible to carry more men and supplies. Unlike the swift caravels, these ships were designed to bring back cargo, not just information.

Columbus's pickings on his four voyages were small, almost insignificant. In fact, at first it seemed that, rather than the westward passage to the Indies, Spain had found a string of islands peopled by half-naked natives. But the country was not about to give up. Continuing the search for a passage to the Indies, Spanish explorers landed in Mexico in 1517. In Yucatan they encountered the Maya Indians, who told them of a rich and powerful empire further north. Unbelievable as it sounds in hindsight, just two years later Hernan Cortez and his ragtag band of conquistadors overran the mighty Aztec empire, beginning the systematic plunder of the great civilizations of South America.

That same year, five vessels left Seville for a voyage to explore the "Great South Sea" that had been sighted across the Panamanian isthmus. The fleet was led by Ferdinand Magellan, who was determined to complete Columbus's quest of reaching the Indies by sailing west. Though Magellan was Portuguese, he knew he could not expect support from his homeland, which already held the keys to the East. Instead he went to Spain, where he obtained backing for the venture.

What followed was a brutal voyage along the coast of South America to the strait that now bears Magellan's name. Once the ships had threaded their way through it, they faced the mightiest ocean on the planet. More than six thousand miles of open seas lay ahead, but Magellan and his crew had no way of knowing that. The voyage took more than three months without provisioning, an ordeal that turned into one of the most appalling passages of the Age of Exploration.

The crew finally found relief in Guam and, a week later, in the Philippines. But there Magellan was killed in a skirmish with a local ruler. His death was untimely and unnecessary, but the expedition had to move on. Though deeply affected by this loss, the survivors realized that Magellan died knowing he had achieved his goal: the East *could* be reached by sailing west.

Three years after setting out from Spain, one vessel, the *Victoria,* returned. Of the original contingent of 240, only eighteen made it back. They were the first men to sail around the world. A hundred years after Henry the Navigator initiated the Age of Exploration, these men completed its crowning voyage, a voyage that proved the earth to be round and gave humanity a sense of its true dimensions.

Spain gained much more than a sense of dimension. By the end of the sixteenth century it ruled an empire that stretched from Europe to the Philippines. From Mexico and later from Peru massive amounts of gold and silver were shipped back in heavily laden treasure galleons. Though many of them fell prey to pirates and sudden storms, enough came through to make Spain the world's wealthiest nation.

Portugal profited from its acquisitions as well, ruthlessly enforcing its monopoly over the East-West spice trade. It succeeded in doing so for much of the sixteenth century, eliminating the Arabs from a trade they had dominated for hundreds of years. But competition soon came from another corner. In 1595 Cornelis de Houtman led the first Dutch voyage to the Moluccas, boldly infringing upon seas that Portugal claimed. Reaching Java, he loaded his ship with pepper and spices, and returned to Holland.

Though nobody knew it at the time, this was the beginning of the end of Portugal's exclusive reign over the eastern trade. Within years the Dutch defeated the Portuguese in India; gained control of Malacca, Sri Lanka, and the Spice Islands; and set up trading stations along the long route to the East. By the mid-seventeenth century, the East Indies trade was firmly under the control of the powerful United East Indies Company.

With the increasing participation of the Dutch, and later the English, in the lucrative East and West Indies trade, ships changed considerably. English and Dutch naval architects had a reputation for being innovative, with the English redrawing the lines of the traditional warship and the Dutch specializing in merchant carriers.

Both nations stepped away from the round-bellied galleons and *naos* favored by Spanish and Portuguese traders, concentrating instead on cleaner lines. Their shipbuilders reduced the size of the high forecastle and placed it aft of the stem, resulting in a ship that was easier to maneuver. They also lowered the stern, and paid more attention to smooth hull forms. For the sail plan, northern shipwrights kept the three masts but

The Iberian voyages of discovery thoroughly changed the world. A cathedral in Goa, India, bears witness of the Portuguese presence in Asia (right). The great civilizations of Central and South America did not survive their confrontation with the Spanish (above).

added sails on the foremast and mainmasts. They also cut the canvas smaller, so that the sails would be easier to handle.

This experimentation resulted not only in a better fighting ship, as the English discovered against the Spanish Armada in 1588, but also in more reliable cargo carriers. Most imposing among these were the Dutch East Indiamen or retour ships that were built specifically for the spice trade in the East Indies. Some of these were the largest vessels afloat, reaching more than one thousand tons. They were well armed, carrying guns on two decks, as well as several hundred sailors and soldiers.

The retour ships were built to be extremely strong, in order to handle a more southerly route to the East Indies. As far as the Cape of Good Hope, the Dutch followed the course pioneered by the Portuguese, giving Africa a wide berth to take advantage of the trade winds. But after putting in at their settlement at Cape Town, the ships continued south. They did not turn until they hit the roaring forties and their galeforce westerlies, which pushed them hard towards the east. After several weeks of "running their easting down," as Dutch seamen came to know the long run, the ships turned north, seeking the southeast trades that took them straight to Batavia and the Spice Islands. Although it was a rough passage, it took only half the time of the old route along the African East Coast and across the Indian Ocean.

SAIL'S LAST STAND

In time the Dutch would lose control of the East Indies trade, replaced by the English and other traders. But the ships that maintained the link between East and West changed relatively little. Some refinements were made to the profile and sail plan, resulting in vessels that were more maneuverable and slightly faster, though not by much. In the late eighteenth century, for instance, Britain's East India Company ships still took from six months to a year to return from the Far East, the same amount of time that they took a hundred years earlier. As long as the company continued to dominate the trade, it saw no compelling reason to make major changes.

Across the Atlantic, there were fewer traditions to stifle ingenuity and innovation. In fact, American ship owners were more interested in speed, and for good reason. During the American Revolutionary War, the rebelling colonies could not hope to match British sea power in traditional ways, which forced them to build fast ships to circumvent both the harsh British laws and the ships that were sent to enforce them. A generation later, during the War of 1812, fast ships again proved essential as privateers and blockade-runners.

What made American ships faster was their knife-like bow, a high length-to-beam ratio, and a V-shaped hull. Some, like the rakish two-masted Chesapeake Bay privateers, became known as Baltimore clippers because they "clipped" the time taken by traditional vessels. After the War of 1812, some of these vessels prospered in the slave trade and other questionable activities where speed was essential. But small clippers also operated in legitimate trades, ferrying cargoes along the coast from one port to another.

It did not take long for the clipper's characteristics to find their way into larger ships as well. Naval architects knew that speed came at the expense of cargo-carrying capacity, but American shippers were no longer willing to wait six months to a year to get their goods from the Far East. In fact, some were even willing to pay premiums to get the year's fresh tea crop on the market earlier. The incentives were sufficiently appealing for ship owners to consider trading cargo capacity for speed.

In response, American shipbuilders began to experiment with traditional hull forms. Donald MacKay of Boston and John W. Griffiths of New York, for instance, incorporated Baltimore clipper characteristics like the sharp bow and V-shaped hull into full-rigged three-masted vessels. Using test tanks to observe water resistance on various hull shapes, they also lengthened the bow and stern, reduced the draft, and increased the beam. Above deck they added lofty masts carrying a massive amount of sail. The result was the true clipper. Some old-timers were convinced that these ships would plow themselves straight to the bottom in a heavy sea, but the results silenced them quickly.

The first two clippers to enter the China trade shaved weeks off the traditional passage. In 1844, the *Houqua* sailed the fifteen thousand miles from Canton to New York via the Cape of Good Hope in an astonishing ninety-five days—sixteen days less than the best previous time. She managed the return leg in ninety days—twenty-three days less than the previous record. The *Rainbow,* launched nine months later, did not do quite as well on her first voyage, but on her second she shattered the return record: eighty-four days from Hong Kong to New York!

More important, from the perspective of the owners, both ships earned more than their construction costs in single voyages. Before long, American shipyards were swamped with orders for clippers, with all of them vying for the distinction of being the fastest clipper from the East. In 1847, John Griffiths's *Sea Witch*, on her first voyage, returned from Hong Kong in eighty-one days. Her second return trip took

Mystic Harbor, Connecticut, provides a splendid reminder of the young American republic's reliance on the sea.

seventy-seven days; the third no more than seventy-four days—a record that has never been broken by a large sailing ship.

American clippers were active in more than the American market. In 1849 the British government repealed the Navigation Act, which had reserved British trade for British ships. Yankee clippers immediately entered the profitable China to London tea trade, and "clipped" the time taken by British vessels by days, and sometimes weeks, cashing in handsomely on the rich premiums offered by London merchants.

But the American success was not destined to last. Before long British shipowners began ordering clippers of their own, to ensure that the Chinese trade would remain in British hands. Built somewhat smaller than their American counterparts, they quickly proved themselves outstanding competitors. Ships like the *Taeping*, the *Ariel*, and the *Serica* became famous throughout the shipping world for their heroics on the long passages home. Some were even able to cash in on that fame. Goods carried on a well-known clipper acquired a glamour that often commanded higher prices.

In spite of increasing competition, there was plenty of work for all. The discovery of gold in California demanded ships, preferably fast ships, to carry gold-crazed men and their supplies from New York around Cape Horn to San Francisco. The *Memnon,* the first clipper to make the West Coast run—took weeks off the traditional travel time for the dangerous fifteen-thousand-mile voyage. Two years later the *Flying Cloud* completed the passage in eighty-nine days, another record that was never surpassed by a

Of the hundreds of clippers built during the mid-nineteenth century, only one survived: the *Cutty Sark*, now permanently berthed in Greenwich near London. Clippers required too much manpower to remain commercially viable.

commercial sailing vessel. Ships like the *Flying Cloud* became legendary, in large part because they had to deal with the worst weather anywhere on earth. But many perished in the fierce storms around Cape Horn, driven to the limit by captains and their "bucko" mates, who refused to shorten sail in their quest for a record passage.

The concurrent discovery of gold in Australia kept the growing contingent of British clippers busy, and here too traditional passage times were shattered. In 1854 the *James Baines* reached Melbourne with seven hundred passengers, fourteen hundred tons of cargo, and three-hundred-and-fifty mailbags after just sixty-three days. Two years later another Black Ball Line vessel, the *Champion of the Seas*, reported sailing four-hundred-and-sixty-five nautical miles in one twenty-four-hour period for an average speed of nearly twenty knots. And in 1866 the *Thermopylae* took barely fifty-nine days on the London to Melbourne run—another passage that still stands firmly in the record books.

Yet by that time, the clipper era was coming to a close. America's clipper fleet suffered a severe economic slump during the late 1850s, and received a final blow during the Civil War, when neutral ships carried much of the trade. British clippers managed to hold on slightly longer, but before long they too found it harder to compete against steam.

The opening of the Suez Canal in 1869 delivered the deathblow. "That dirty ditch," sailing-ship captains called it, and for good reason. The canal brought the Far East within range of steamships, thereby halving the time clippers took on their passage

around South Africa. With time more and more of the essence, it was impossible for clippers to compete. A few of them continued to make their way to China, but not for long.

Clippers had to seek employment elsewhere. For some time they made their mark in the Australian wool trade, racing back from Sydney with wool for England's textile mills—a trip they regularly completed in less than three months. But these were the clippers' last achievements. With their large crews they became increasingly expensive to operate, and every year steam was gaining. By the 1880s only a handful of clippers remained.

Even so, sail put up a hard battle in its struggle to survive. Giant steel-hulled windjammers—the largest sailing vessels ever—began to appear, carrying bulk goods like nitrates from Chili; grains from Australia; and, ironically, coal from Wales and Australia to bunkering stations around the world. Much larger than the swift clippers, windjammers took more or less the same size crew to operate; simpler rigging saw to that. They also carried considerably more cargo: up to three or four times as much. These economies of scale enabled them to survive well into the twentieth century.

In this final stand of commercial sail, the fleet of Hamburg owner Ferdinand Laeisz raised the operation of sailing ships to a new level. Using huge vessels captained by handpicked men, the Laeisz fleet took general cargo from Hamburg to Valparaiso and returned with nitrate from ports further north. Used for fertilizers and munitions, nitrate was one of the most profitable cargoes of the time, though it was noxious and flammable. And the trip was nastier still, around Cape Horn, even in winter, in the worst of its notoriously bad weather.

Some of the most heroic passages in the story of the sea were written aboard these ships. It is fashionable to look at these last days of the age of sail as romantic, but the accounts of people like Alan Villiers and Irving Johnson show how little romance existed for those involved in these voyages, except perhaps in hindsight. Hundreds of sailors were swept overboard or fell from the rigging; ships regularly perished with all aboard. It was a brutal trade that many ship owners were relieved to see disappear forever.

The end of World War II triggered a phenomenal expansion of world trade, but not for sail. By then, the working Western sailing ship had all but disappeared, unable to compete with its engine-driven counterparts.

Fortunately sail was not discarded altogether. Some nations held onto a few tall ships to train young people, recognizing how valuable a passage on a square-rigger is in showing a mariner what is needed at sea. Elsewhere people began to realize the importance of safeguarding the last survivors. They raised funds, bought, and often lovingly restored abandoned ships. Now many ports and maritime museums throughout the world proudly display a tall ship of their own, to remind people of what once was, and to ensure that they will not disappear.

And that seems only right because these ships represent the crowning glory of thousands of years of sail development. More importantly, they symbolize the teamwork, ingenuity, and courage that were required to survive at sea. And that should never be forgotten.

The Portuguese naval training vessel *Sagres* in the Caribbean. The square sails on the foremast and the mainmast reveal it to be a bark.

WESTERN VESSEL TYPES

Providing an overview of Western sailing vessels is a challenge because there are so many of them. Other cultures too possessed a wide diversity of ships, but they at least tended to retain some continuity throughout the centuries, making the task somewhat more manageable. In the West, in contrast, the constant experimentation with hull forms and rigging created a far greater number of possible variations. Unlike the method used for vessels of other cultures, the classification of Western ships tends to be based on rigging configuration. As a result, ships belonging to the same vessel type may be quite different in size and hull shape.

Since a number of classic Western sailing craft were preserved (or rebuilt) for exhibition, sail training, or cruising, there are still opportunities to see these vessels where they belong: at sea. Among the most important were (and are) the following types:

Bark
A three-masted sailing ship, square-rigged on the foremast and mainmast, and fore- and aft-rigged on the mizzen. The larger four- and five-masted barks similarly were square-rigged on all but the aftermost mast. Barks in the tall ship fleet include the *Alexander von Humboldt* (1906), *Belem* (1896), *Cuauhtemoc* (1982), *Eagle* (1936), *Elissa* (1877), *Europa* (1911), *Gloria* (1968), *Gorch Fock II* (1958), *Guayas* (1977), *Kaskelot* (1948), *Mircea* (1938), *Sagres* (1937), *Simon Bolivar* (1980), *Statsraad Lehmkuhl* (1914), and *Tovarishch* (1933). Examples of four-masted barks include the *Kruzenshtern* (ex Padua) (1926), *Sedov* (1921), and the newer *Nippon Maru II* and *Kaiwo Maru II*, both built in the 1980s for the Institute of Sea Training in Japan.

Barkentine

Similar to the bark, but square-rigged only on the foremast and fore-and-aft rigged on all others. Barkentines that can still be seen include *Atlantis* (1905), *Dewaruci* (1952), *Gazela* (1883; the oldest wooden square-rigged ship still operational), *Mercator* (1932), *Regina Maris* (1908), and *Esmeralda* (1952; with four masts the largest of all).

Brig

Generally speaking a brig was a two-masted vessel that was square-rigged on both masts, with an additional gaff and boom sail on the mainmast. Since the brig is an older vessel type, most brigs in the current tall ship fleet are either replicas or new-builts. They include *Aphrodite* (1994), *Astrid* (1918), *Fryderyk Chopin* (1992), *Niagara* (1988), and *Royalist* (1971).

Brigantine

A two-masted ship, square-rigged on the foremast and fore-and-aft rigged on the mainmast. Fore-and-aft rigging generally took less crew, so this was more of a trading vessel, whereas brigs were usually found in government service. Sometimes brigantines are known as hermaphrodite brigs. Examples include *Corwith Cramer* (1987), *Eye of the Wind* (1911), and *Søren Larsen* (1949).

Clipper

Technically speaking clippers are ship-rigged vessels (see below), but they came to describe the sleek, fast square-rigged ships of the middle of the nineteenth century with their raking stem and overhanging stern. It is said they developed from the smaller two-masted Baltimore clippers, of which one has been rebuilt: the *Pride of Baltimore II*, a frequent participant in tall ship events. The clippers proper were three-masted vessels, though one—the towering *Great Republic*—was built with four. Only one true clipper survives: the *Cutty Sark,* now permanently berthed in Greenwich, England. Among tall ship participants, the recently built *Stad Amsterdam* (2000) comes closest to approximating the form of a true clipper.

Schooner

Schooners started out as two-masted, fore-and-aft rigged vessels, with a foremast shorter than the mainmast. During the nineteenth century, they came to include all fore-and-aft rigged vessels, regardless of the number of masts, as long as the first one was not taller than the others. Schooners served in a wide variety of functions, from lumber carriers to Grand Banks fishing vessels, fast coastal traders, and later pleasure craft as well. As a result, there is an immense variety in shape and form in the current schooner fleet, which includes *American Eagle* (1930),

The American *Corwith Cramer*, here seen on the Chesapeake Bay, is an example of a brigantine.

Bluenose II (1963), *Bowdoin* (1921), *Creoula* (1937), *Elinor* (1906), *Ernestina* (1894), *Lettie G. Howard* (1893), *Shendandoah* (1902), and replicas like *Lady Maryland* (1986). Staysail schooners were built for speed and set large triangular sails on and between their masts; an example is the *Creole* (1927). Gaff schooners, in contrast, were cargo carriers, rigged with easier-to-handle gaff sails. They operated throughout the world, from the islands of the Caribbean to the North Sea, where Holland's *Zeelandia* (1931) can still regularly be seen.

Topsail schooner

Also initially a two-masted vessel, fore-and-aft rigged on both masts, with the exception of the top foremast that carries one or more square sails. Only a few traditional topsail schooners survive, among them the *Alexandria* (1929), *Marité* (1923), and *Oosterschelde* (1918). New-builts include the Japanese *Akogare* (1993) and *Californian* (1984), a replica of a nineteenth-century Revenue Cutter. The largest topsail schooner in the tall ship fleet is Spain's *Juan Sebastian de Elcano* (1927).

Ship

The proper definition of a ship in (Western) nautical terms is a vessel with at least three masts, all of them square-rigged, with a gaff on the mizzen and a bowsprit. These requirements made for labor-intensive ships, requiring large crews. Clippers were ship-rigged, as were most large warships of the eighteenth-century, like frigates and ships of the line. The tall ship fleet includes many ship-rigged vessels, among them veteran sail-training ships like *Amerigo Vespucci* (1931), *Christian Radich*

(1937), *Danmark* (1933), and *Georg Stage* (1935); and more recent additions like *Khersones* (1987), *Libertad* (1960), and *Mir* (1987).

Historic ship types that are no longer to be seen, except in a few instances as replicas or museum exhibits, include the following:

Caravel
A southern European trading and exploration vessel, which proved its value and seaworthiness during the first European voyages of exploration to Africa and the New World. It was originally lateen-rigged to improve its windward ability, a design that came to be known as a *caravela latina*. For longer distances square sails were rigged on the foremast and mainmast; then the ship was known as a *caravela redonda* or *rotunda*. Two *caravelas* were rebuilt in Portugal in the late 1980s, to commemorate the 500th anniversary of Bartolomeu Dias's voyage around the Cape of Good. Both are now exhibited in museums.

Carrack
A large trading vessel that appeared on European waters in the fourteenth century, first as a two-masted vessel with a large square sail on the mainmast and a lateen sail on the mizzen. The demand for additional cargo space in the fifteenth century led to a much larger carrack and another mast—a square-rigged foremast, resulting in a forerunner of sorts of the classic Western three-masted vessel. Like cogs, the workhorse cargo carriers of the Middle Ages, carracks had high fore-and-aft castles, which made them difficult to sail in adverse winds.

Cog
The principal merchant ship of northern Europe from the thirteenth to fifteenth centuries. Cogs had one mast, which set a large square sail, as well as fore- and aft-castles that made them useful for military purposes as well. They had a broad beam, and were clinker-built either with a rounded or a relatively sharp bow. Some cog replicas have now been built in Germany and the Netherlands, their measurements based on the preserved hulls of wrecks.

Fluyt
A Dutch merchantman of the seventeenth century, with a round stern narrowing towards the poop, creating an inward slope on either side. The ship had three masts, conventionally rigged for the time, that is, square sails on the foremast and mainmast and a lateen on the mizzen. Though far less impressive than the Dutch East Indiamen, fluyts played an equally important role in the Dutch economy, servicing the European and especially the Baltic trades.

Galleon
A logical development from the carrack, wherein English shipbuilders lowered the carrack's high forecastle to create a ship that was easier to steer and sail. Galleons played an important role in the British defeat of the Spanish Armada. Convinced of their usefulness, the Spanish began to build galleons themselves, which they used on their East and West Indies trades.

Galley
Usually known as an oared vessel from ancient times, galleys continued to operate in European waters until well into the eighteenth century. Unlike their predecessors, which carried a square sail and several rows of oarsman, the later Mediterranean galley was lateen-rigged. Eventually the oars were changed to a single row to reduce the number of people required aboard. Oared vessels with higher topsides became knows as galleasses. They regularly sailed from the Mediterranean into the Atlantic, carrying products from Italian city-states like Venice and Genoa to northern European ports.

Lugger
A working vessel used either for fishing or coastal trade, with two or three masts rigged with lugsails: fore-and-aft-like sails not unlike the gaff sails seen on three-masted ships of the eighteenth and nineteenth centuries. The lugger is different in that the spar (or lug) crosses the mast, whereas a gaff always fits snugly to the mast.

EPILOGUE

This book is entitled *Setting Sail* for two reasons. On the one hand it is about sailing, or rather the history of sail. But setting sail has a transitive meaning as well: the sails are being set, and in many cases they are being set permanently. In that sense, this book also represents a tribute. After thousands of years the era of commercial sail is coming to a close. Of course, it started doing so the moment steam engines began to replace masts and rigging in the mid- to late-nineteenth century. But sail held on, in some areas for another fifty or even one hundred years, and in a few places until today. It probably will not hold on for too much longer.

People interested in maritime history tend to see this happen with a tinge of regret. After all, commercial sail's disappearance represents the end of an era. Pages are turned over all the time, but we are not just witnessing the disappearance of a ship—of something that gets us or a cargo from one place to another. These ships also came to symbolize what it took to operate them: courage, teamwork and discipline—values well worth remembering, and not only at sea.

In just the same way that our interaction with the sea was recorded to varying degrees in different areas, there are regional differences in people's perception of what should be remembered or preserved, and how to go about that. Polynesia was described in this book as a region of great voyagers: an area where people navigated enormous distances at sea long before others dared to do so. Unfortunately these people did not record their achievements other than in their oral tradition. And unfortunately their descendants initially did not show much of an inclination to preserve what was left of that, or a great deal else for that matter.

To be fair, that was not entirely their fault. Western teachers and missionaries did a very effective job of convincing people in Polynesia that their oral tradition was, if not irrelevant, then at least largely imagined and thus useless from a historical perspective. Waka (canoe) traditions and genealogies that had been passed on for many generations were forgotten, or were altered by new information: geographical, pseudo-historical, or even religious. Many Polynesians lost pride in their roots and culture, and readily accepted whatever the West thought appropriate.

As a result, preservation was never a priority. Traditional vessels survived well into the twentieth century, but when they disappeared no one seemed to notice or care. After all, these craft represented what was said to be a backward culture. Fishermen and others readily gave up their outriggers for synthetic materials and outboards. Today one is hard-pressed to find signs or remnants of that great maritime tradition when traveling throughout Polynesia.

Fortunately the situation has been changing. It took a first major turn for the better in the early 1970s when a small group of Hawaiians—Western and native—took up the idea of rebuilding one of the great Hawaiian voyaging canoes of the eleventh or twelfth century. Of course, no one knew what a great voyaging canoe of that era would have looked like. Neither the early Hawaiians nor the Tahitians had left behind any useful pictures, and the chance of ever finding a wreck was essentially non-existent for the simple reason that their craft (unlike displacement hulls) never sank; instead they just broke up at sea. But even in the absence of pictures or prototypes, the replica builders were not deterred. They carefully studied the notes and drawings left by later Western explorers, and extrapolated a generic eastern Polynesian design that was given the name *Hokule'a*—the Hawaiian name for Arcturus, the islands' zenith star.

Though no one knew whether *Hokule'a* could be considered a faithful replica, her 1975 launch represented the onset of a transformation in the way Polynesians perceived their maritime heritage. Under the aegis of the newly founded Polynesian Voyaging Society, *Hokule'a* began to make voyages: first small ones to neighboring islands, and then, in 1976, a long one to Tahiti, which confirmed that Polynesian voyaging canoes were sturdy and capable (though not necessarily comfortable) vessels. Moreover, the skills of Satawalese navigator Mau Pialiug demonstrated that these vessels could be guided over long distances without a complement of Western navigational instruments. Four years later *Hokule'a* redid the voyage, this time with Nainoa Thompson, a young Hawaiian who had studied under Mau Pialiug, as navigator. An epic 16,000-mile journey followed in 1985-87 that took the canoe through much of the central and western Pacific, and as far south as New Zealand.

These voyages not only taught historians and experimental archaeologists a great deal about Polynesian seafaring, they also struck a deep chord with native Hawaiians, who began to take a far greater interest in their past. At times this took on political overtones, which would not have been the original intention, but in general this renewed interest proved a healthy, and even contagious development. Before long, people on other Polynesian islands began to construct canoe replicas of their own—some more accurate than others—and began to train young people in non-instrument navigation to ensure that this tradition would not be lost. Today there are several replicas in operation, most of which have undertaken long ocean passages. They include the Cook Islands' *Takitumu, Ngapuariki,* and *Te Au Tonga; Te Aurere* from New Zealand; and, besides *Hokule'a* herself, *Hawailoa, Makalii,* and *E'ala* from the Hawaiian Islands.

Aside from the powerful symbolic impact left by these replicas, there also are several excellent museums, especially in Hawaii and New Zealand, which focus on Polynesian seafaring and seem committed to ensuring that this heritage will no longer be allowed to reach the point of extinction. Of course, the further one moves from the centers of tourism and

Throughout Southeast Asia, it is still possible to encounter small traditional vessels.

development, the more modest the resources, but several of the smaller islands have taken initiatives as well to preserve seafaring skills and technologies, thereby giving people a chance to take pride in them.

Even further away, well beyond the outline of the Polynesian triangle, there still are opportunities to encounter small-scale traditional practices. As a general rule, the further removed one is from places with a lot of money, the greater the chance of finding something original, not because people there are so intent on preserving it, but because they have no choice. Thus in the islands of the Philippines and Indonesia, among them the probable home islands of the original Austronesian voyagers, fishermen still take to the sea in small single and double outriggers, equipped with a rag-tag triangular sail, much the same way their ancestors did for thousands of years. They would probably prefer an easier-to-maintain fiberglass boat with a sturdy outboard, but they do not have the money for that. It seems almost fortunate that it is still that way, though the fishermen themselves may well beg to differ.

Also along the so-called Lapita corridor, and especially in the islands north of New Guinea, there still are some traditional vessels. They are rapidly disappearing, however, and with them the ability to construct and maintain them. In places such as the Reef Santa Cruz islands and Taumako in the Duff Group (Solomons), efforts are underway to prevent this knowledge from disappearing. It takes a bit of help from developed nations for this to proceed but, judging from the experience in Hawaii and elsewhere, it is well worth the investment.

There are some interesting parallels between Polynesia and the Indian Ocean region. Here too the rule applies that the further one is located from centers of tourism and money, the greater the likelihood of finding something original. The best chances exist along the East African coast south of Zanzibar, especially in Mozambique, and further north along the Kenyan coast north of Lamu. In the central coastal region as well, many small dhows are used for fishing, or increasingly to ferry tourists to outlying beaches. In fact, it may well be the phenomenal growth of tourism that guarantees the survival of the dhow in this area. Of course, tourists will eventually require something more comfortable, with a cover, for instance, or adequate seating, but with a little luck what develops may still resemble a dhow.

In the outlying areas dhows survive for the simple reason that fuel is expensive and the wind is free. As a result, small dhows will continue to ferry people and cargoes along the coast for some time to come. Preservation is not a priority here, so some of the larger dhows will disappear once they are abandoned. These losses are unfortunate, but without some outside help, not a great deal can be expected. Here, too, help may materialize as tourism extends its reaches further north and south along the East African coast, at first because people will find out that they can make money taking tourists on small trips; and later because they begin to realize that these vessels represent a direct link with their past, and are thus essential to their cultural identity.

Across the Indian Ocean, along the coast of India and Sri Lanka, there are still a few large sailing dhows. They also face difficulties surviving because they require a lot of

In East Africa, sailing dhows remain a vital part of life along the coast.

manpower. *Kotia, thoni,* and other large sailing dhows will eventually become commercially unviable and few, if any, plans for preserving them exist among people who have more pressing concerns. Smaller (motorized) dhows, on the other hand, still continue to be built, especially along the Gujarati coast, and will continue to play a role in coastal waters for some time to come.

Along the Arabian peninsula, sailing dhows have all but disappeared, with the exception of Yemen's Red Sea coast. Yemen possesses oil reserves, though nothing comparable to those of its neighbors. As a result fuel remains relatively expensive, leading a good number of Yemeni *sambuks* and other dhows to retain a small mast and sail to make use of favorable winds. On the other side of the Red Sea, in Djibouti and Eritrea, many fishing and small trading dhows, though equipped with small inboard or outboard engines, are able to take advantage of a good breeze.

Elsewhere in the Arabian peninsula fuel is so inexpensive that it does not make economic sense to retain a mast and rigging, and especially the extra manpower needed. Even so, dhows remain a familiar sight because many fishermen and small merchant ship owners seem to prefer wooden hulls. This tradition has kept numerous wooden dhow yards in operation along the shores of the Arabian peninsula, even in the wealthiest oil states.

The resources created by the oil boom permit preservation, which is now beginning to be applied to the region's nautical heritage. Several maritime museums and exhibits exist, especially around the Persian Gulf. A number of working dhows have been preserved in Kuwait, Qatar, and Oman. Preservation efforts range from those undertaken by the people of Sur in Oman to preserve one of their *ganjahs* to the admirable grassroots effort of the fishermen of Al Hami in Yemen to preserve one of their *sambuk*-like sailing dhows. Conditions for preservation—sometimes a beach, elsewhere a lagoon or a quay—are not necessarily optimal, but the practice reflects a growing interest in preserving maritime history and publicizing its role in the region.

Few replicas of the great sailing dhows of the past have been built, with the exception of a magnificent three-masted sailing dhow owned by Sultan Qaboos of Oman, and a few vessels commissioned by wealthy merchant families. Among them is *Al Hashiri II*, at 250 feet the largest wooden dhow in the world. A giant replica of a *baggala*, this vessel is dry-docked in Kuwait, serving as conference center and maritime museum. Staying a bit more true to the dhow's original function, the Omani government financed the reconstruction of *Sohar*, a replica of a ninth-century China trading dhow, which actually retraced the entire voyage under sail in the early 1980s. The vessel is currently displayed in the middle of a traffic circle not far from the Omani capital of Muscat. Though both the rotary and the vessel are immaculately maintained, the ship would benefit from a different location. But neither the size of Oman's population nor the number of visitors justifies the expense of a permanent exhibit. This is unfortunate because *Sohar* probably represents the best example of one of the trading dhows of the golden age of Arab seafaring.

Depending on the region and its resources, more attention is thus slowly being paid to preserving the dhow and its heritage. In some cases it is evidenced by the first attempts at ship preservation and dedicated maritime exhibits; in others by a growing interest in sailing new-built dhows, as is the case with dhow racing in the United Arab Emirates, for instance. Still, many of these efforts face a difficult time garnering support and attention because public interest remains low. In time this may change, as the Arabs begin to rediscover the important role ships played in their history and their religion, and as they begin to realize that this role provides ample reason for pride.

If Middle Eastern preservation efforts are hampered by a lack of interest, the situation is even more of a challenge in China. Like much of the Middle East, China pursued maritime ambitions only during certain times in her history, most of these long ago and long forgotten, it seems. Public interest in maritime history is virtually non-existent, and maritime education and preservation, as a consequence, lag far behind. In addition maritime occupations do not carry great social status, another indication that China has some way to go before its population takes more of an interest in the sea and its role in her history.

Nonetheless, some changes are taking place. China is becoming a serious maritime contender, with a strong navy and modern merchant fleet, and a growing realization that it cannot achieve its global ambition without an adequate maritime presence. These factors may promote a more sea-minded attitude among the public at large. China is also becoming a far wealthier nation. Though its priorities are still oriented towards large-scale development, in time this will enable the country to take stock of its maritime heritage and decide what should be preserved. The country's small but active Marine History Research Association, based in Shanghai, is quite active in this regard. While it remains a lone voice in the desert, or in this case at sea, some progress has been made.

The best Chinese maritime museums and exhibits were added recently. With the return of Hong Kong and Macau, for instance, the excellent Macau Maritime Museum and the various shipping-related exhibits in Hong Kong's Science and History Museums became part of the country's educational resources. Though these were started and

China is only slowly taking more of an interest in maritime history.

156

developed under their respective colonial administrations, reflecting Portugal and Britain's particular interests in maritime history, they continue to fare well. In fact, current Hong Kong Chief Executive C. H. Tung has strong maritime credentials, having been in charge of a container carrier. In early 2003 he opened the C.Y. Tung Maritime Museum in Shanghai in memory of his father, who founded a major shipping company and had a deep interest in Chinese maritime history. Though most Chinese do not share that interest yet, this type of effort is a step in the right direction.

Even so, many steps remain to be taken. The important Ming voyages of the early fifteenth century, without question a high point in world maritime history, hardly get any exposure. There is a small Zheng He Memorial Hall in Liuhe, near the mouth of the Yangtze River, but it seems to be known only by those already interested in the topic, or by local schoolchildren, who have no choice. Near Nanjing's Jin-Lan temple is a small museum that supposedly keeps some of the artifacts recovered from the nearby Ming Dynasty shipyards, but their condition does not promise a long existence. Besides, most of what was found in the former shipbuilding docks was burned by local farmers to heat their huts or warm up their meals. Quanzhou in Fujian province, once one of the great trading ports, is one of the few cities with a dedicated maritime museum. Not far from the main hall the museum exhibits the re-assembled hull of the Quanzhou ship, the wreck of a Song Dynasty trader that was found in the area some thirty years ago. Whether the hull will survive the next thirty years remains to be seen, however. The wood, which is badly in need of treatment, will start to crumble unless it is immersed in a preservation solution, a process that will take years and considerable money.

A number of wrecks from the Song and Yuan dynasties have also been excavated in northern China, Thailand (Pattaya), and Korea (Wando and Shinan), and many more no doubt await discovery. The Korean finds are undergoing proper conservation treatment prior to display. Korea also has several maritime museums that, though modest by Western standards, reflect a relatively strong public interest in the sea and its history. Perhaps this is not surprising, given the phenomenal growth in the country's maritime capabilities.

Further east lies Japan, now also a formidable maritime power. The country cannot look back on a great maritime past, having been forced into several periods of isolation, the most important of which coincided with the Western European oceanic break-out. Still, maritime history and education are well promoted in Japan, with several high quality maritime museums, a number of historic ships, and a level of public sea-mindedness other nations can only dream of.

This type of broad effort provides people with a context and stimulates public interest in things nautical. For the time being this context is lacking in China. That can and may be turned around, the way it already has elsewhere, but it will require a dedicated effort. Not only would the Chinese benefit, so would maritime history because much of the story of China and the sea is worth knowing about and preserving.

The West, in contrast, has nurtured the conditions that support preservation of a nautical heritage. Not only was the West far more diligent in recording its interaction with ships and the sea throughout the centuries, it also followed up on that by preserving it. Nowhere in the world are there so many maritime museums, historic ships, historic ship replicas, and maritime events as there are in Europe and North America. This, of course, has something to do with affluence. Preservation is usually considered a luxury, at least when compared with basic needs. It can be argued that some tangible recollections of the past are as essential to a culture as food and water are to an individual, but when there is no choice, that becomes a moot point.

Yet affluence isn't the only factor at work. After all, this business of preserving or rebuilding ships, and exhibiting them and nautical artifacts in museums, is a relatively new phenomenon. No one ever thought of expressly preserving one of the many American clippers that were built in the mid-nineteenth century, for instance. As a result, not a single one survived. Most of the ships that made it into the historic ship fleet got there by chance, by simply surviving long enough, in whatever shape, for people to realize their value. And people did not really begin to do so until the second half of the twentieth century.

Even so, there is no question that Westerners have taken more of an interest in their maritime heritage than others. It is worth trying to figure out why this is the case. Perhaps it has to do with timing. The great age of Western sail indeed unfolded more recently than similar eras elsewhere. The Polynesians' great sea exploits took place between twenty-five hundred and twelve hundred years ago; in the case of the Arabs we have to go back more than one thousand years; and for the Chinese more than five hundred. In each case these periods of intense activity were followed by a long period of inactivity. Western sail reached its zenith much later, and it lasted until much more recently. In fact, until seventy years ago, less than a lifetime, the last remnants of that great age of sail could still be seen at sea carrying commercial cargoes. And the ships live on year after year through the tall ship events held regularly at American and European ports.

In addition, this period of oceanic expansion had an enormous impact because it was accompanied by a massive movement of people. When the Ming emperors sent out their fleets, they did not do so with the intent of colonizing other regions. The Arabs too dispatched merchants and sailors, not large groups of emigrants. It is possible that ships figure more prominently in the Western psyche because so much of North America's population has ancestors who arrived there by ship. Many people in Europe saw part of the family leave for overseas. Ships thus were not only impersonal carriers of trade, they also carried families to a new life and personally affected innumerable people. They were the first links in a shrinking world, in what we now call the global village.

Finally, perhaps size matters here. The last stage in Western commercial sail development was a very impressive ship. They are somewhat unimaginatively referred to as tall ships, but they are more like cathedrals, towering high above us. We look up to them as we do cathedrals, literally as well as figuratively, because they symbolize something larger than us. Perhaps it goes against the essence of much of this book, but a Western square-rigger looks a great deal more impressive than a junk, a dhow, or a Polynesian voyaging canoe for that matter. This does not mean they are better or more ingenious, but it does imply that they are likely to elicit a stronger reaction. Assemble a fleet of them and invariably tens or hundreds of thousands of people, sometimes even millions, flock together to take a look at them. What brings them there? A ship? Or something more?

I suspect it is something more. A personal perception is involved because these ships correspond to an image of beauty and majesty, but there is also something a bit more abstract, or even subconscious, at work. It is as though we assemble to pay tribute. To the way these ships shaped the world and much of history. To the courage and bravery that it took to operate them. And to the recognition that they allowed us to master something enormous (the ocean) with limited means (a ship)—an undertaking that required ingenuity, teamwork, and discipline.

These are timeless values indeed. And if the old sailing ships can help us remember them, they deserve all the love and respect we have bestowed on them.

ACKNOWLEDGMENTS

This book was some time in the making for a variety of reasons. For one thing, the maritime history of some regions covered in the book is not exactly blessed with much literature. As a result, the draft sometimes just sat there for a while, until I found something else that could be incorporated. In spite of this long gestation period, the result remains no more than a very broad overview. If errors and inaccuracies crept in, the responsibility is mine.

In due time, the draft became associated with plans for a documentary film series. The two became closely related and also benefited from one another. Hence it is appropriate to thank some of the people involved in the production. Admittedly people in television already do a good job of acknowledging themselves in credits that go as far as listing drivers and whoever made the sandwiches that morning. We usually make our own sandwiches, so I'll keep it short.

Films like the ones associated with this book cost a lot of money and in a documentary television world which appears far more interested in mummies and crocodiles (or preferably both), it takes strong-minded individuals to green-light a production that focuses on world maritime history. Strong initial support came from NHK, Japan's public broadcaster, where Kagari Tajima, then affiliated with the co-production office, and Executive Producers Nobuo Isobe and Etsuzo Yamazaki made sure everything could proceed under optimal conditions. NHK not only made funds and equipment available; it also provided excellent on-line editing and audio mixing staff and facilities.

It was difficult to figure out who was in charge of co-production at RTP, Portugal's public broadcaster, but producer Alice Milheiro unquestionably played an instrumental role. Alice not only got us our crews when and where we needed them, she also made sure the contract got signed. Given the fact that this didn't take place until long after the production was finished, her contribution is even more impressive. At VRT, the Flemish public broadcasting organization, Frans Lefever moved things along. Unlike its Portuguese counterpart, VRT doesn't release funds or facilities until all the *T*'s are crossed, and we are grateful to Frans for making sure this took place prior to production.

The creative teams for this type of documentary can become substantial. We didn't have the funds for a large crew, so here the list is mercifully short: Fernando Lourenço and Vasco Riobom on camera, João Martinho and Mick Sawaguchi for respectively field sound and final mix; Guy Cuyvers for the orchestral score; John Vermilye for the English-language narration and Kaye Gustafson and Saika Otake on production management. They all did a splendid job, in spite of occasionally less than optimal conditions.

We were fortunate to have access to some top experts. Inevitably some of their contributions seeped into the book, so it is appropriate to acknowledge their assistance: Dr. Glenn Summerhayes of the Australian National University; Prof. Roger Green, Dr. Rawiri Taonui and Dr. Geoffrey Irwin, all from the University of Auckland; Dr. Yosihiko Sinoto of the Bishop Museum in Honolulu, Hawaii; Dr. Sergio Rapu, Hanga Roa, Easter Island; Dr. Alan Ziegler, Honolulu; and Dr. Ben Finney and Dr. Barry Rolett of the University of Hawaii.

Chapter 2 and Program 2 benefited from the insight of Dr. Nadia Lokma of the Egyptian Museum in Cairo; Douglas Haldane of the Institute of Nautical Archaeology in Alexandria; Dr. Roberto Orazi of the National Research Council in Rome; Prof. Isam Al-Rawas and Prof. Mohammed Said Al Muqudam of the Sultan Qaboos University in

Oman; Said Nasser Ali Al Salmi of Oman's Ministry of Information; and Dr. Joseph Cheruiyot of the Lamu Museum, Kenya.

The Chinese story presented in Chapter 3 and Program 3 was clarified by Prof. Mai Yinghao, Chief Archaeologist in Guangzhou; Dr. Li Guo Qing of the Museum of Overseas Communication History in Quanzhou; Dr. Luo Zongzhen of the Nanjing Museum; and the late Prof. Osamu Oba. Similarly the Western side of the story benefited from the participation of Prof. Christos Doumas, Chief Archaeologist of the Archaeological Site of Akrotiri; Dr. Dimitris Kourkoumelis of the Ephorate of Underwater Antiquities in Athens; Tinna Damgård Sørensen of the Viking Ship Museum in Roskilde, Denmark; Jean-Pierre Van Roeyen of the Archaeologische Dienst Waasland, Belgium; Dr. Gustaaf Asaert, Antwerp; Commander Estacio dos Reis, Biblioteca Central da Marinha in Lisbon; Diederik Wildeman of the Nederlands Scheepvaart Museum in Amsterdam; Caroline Hampton and Pieter van der Merwe from the National Maritime Museum in Greenwich; Melbourne Smith of the International Historical Watercraft Society in Annapolis, MD; and Peter Neill of the South Street Seaport Museum in New York.

Books and films need access to locations, and I would like to acknowledge some of the organizations that provided the necessary permissions: the National Research Institute, Papua New Guinea; the Papua New Guinea National Museum; the Auckland Museum; Samoa Visitors Bureau; the Parque Nacional Rapa Nui; the Polynesian Voyaging Society; the Polynesian Cultural Center; the Egyptian Museum, Cairo; the Solar Ship Museum, Giza; the Supreme Council of Antiquities, Cairo; the Institute of Nautical Archaeology; the Ministry of Information, Oman; the National Museums of Kenya; the Jiangsu Provincial Government and Provincial Tourism Administration; the Quanzhou Maritime Museum; the Guangdong Museum; the Nanjing Museum; the Mongol Invasion Memorial Hall, Fukuoka; the Takashima Municipal Museum; the Guangzhou Historical Museum; the Matsuura Historical Museum, Hirado; the Archaeological Museum, Athens; the National Maritime Museum, Greenwich; the Nederlands Scheepvaart Museum, Amsterdam; the Hellenic Maritime Museum, Piraeus; the Viking Ship Museum, Roskilde; the Museu da Marinha, Lisbon; the Nationaal Scheepvaart Museum, Antwerp; the Mariners Museum, Newport News; and the South Street Seaport Museum, New York.

Finally a tip of the hat to the people who made this book possible. Carolyn Wilcox showed a great deal of skill and patience in getting the manuscript into the proper shape, while Bart Luijten of B2 Communications took care of the design. My sincere appreciation also goes to publisher Scott Kaeser and the staff at Tide-mark Press for making this book available to the North American market.

BIBLIOGRAPHY

THE GREAT VOYAGERS

Banks, Joseph. *The Endeavour Journal, Vols. I and II*. Sydney: Angus & Robertson, 1962.

Barthel, Thomas S. *The Eighth Land: The Polynesian Discovery and Settlement of Easter Island*. Honolulu: University of Hawaii Press, 1978.

Beckwith, Martha W. (ed. and tr.). 1981. Reprint. *The Kumulipo, A Hawaiian Creation Chant*. Chicago: The University of Chicago Press, 1951.

_____. *Hawaiian Mythology*. 1970. Reprint. Honolulu: University of Hawaii Press, 1940.

Bellwood, Peter S. *Man's Conquest of the Pacific*. Auckland: Collins, 1978.

Buck, Peter H. (Te Rangi Hiroa). *Vikings of the Pacific*. Chicago: University of Chicago Press, 1959.

Cook, James, J. C. Beaglehole, (ed.), and R. A. Skelton (ed.). *The Journals of Captain James Cook on his Voyages of Discovery. Vol. III. The Voyage of the Resolution and Discovery: 1776-1780*. Cambridge (Engl.): Hakluyt Society, 1967.

Corney, Bolton G. (ed.). *The Quest and Occupation of Tahiti by Emissaries of Spain during the Years 1772-1776*. London: Hakluyt Society, 1913-1919.

Dodd, Edward. *Polynesian Seafaring*. New York: Dodd, Mead, 1972.

Feinberg, Richard. *Polynesian Seafaring and Navigation: Ocean Travel in Anutan Culture and Society*. Kent, Ohio: Kent State University Press, 1988.

Finney, Ben. *Hokule'a: The Way to Tahiti*. New York, Dodd, Mead, 1979.

_____. "Nautical Cartography and Traditional Navigation in Oceania." In *The History of Cartography*, Vol. 2, Book 3: *Cartography in the Traditional African, American, Arctic, Australian, and Pacific Societies*, ed. by David Woodward and G. Malcolm Lewis. Chicago: The University of Chicago Press, 1998.

_____. *Voyage of Rediscovery*. Berkeley: University of California Press, 1994.

_____. "Voyaging and Isolation in Rapa Nui Prehistory." *Rapa Nui Journal*, Vol. 7, No. 1 (March 1993).

Goldman, Irving. *Ancient Polynesian Society*. Chicago: The University of Chicago Press, 1970.

Green, Roger C. "New Information for the Ferry Berth Site, Mulifanua, Western Samoa." *Pacific Studies*, Vol. 12, No. 3 (July 1989), pp. 319-329.

Grey, George. 1988. Reprint. *Legends of Aotearoa*. Hamilton, N.Z.: Silver Fern Books, 1885.

Hill, Adrian V. S., and Susan W. Serjeantson (eds.). *The Colonization of the Pacific: A Genetic Trail*. Oxford: Clarendon Press, 1989.

Howells, W. W. *The Pacific Islanders*. London: Weidenfeld & Nicolson, 1973.

Irwin, Geoffrey. *The Prehistoric Exploration and Colonization of the Pacific*. Cambridge (Engl.): Cambridge University Press, 1992.

Jennings, Jesse D. (ed.). *The Prehistory of Polynesia*. Cambridge, Mass.: Harvard University Press, 1979.

Kane, Herb Kawainui. *Ancient Hawaii*. Honolulu: The Kawainui Press, 1997.

Kirch, Patrick. *Feathered Gods and Fishhooks: An Introduction to Hawaiian Archaeology and Prehistory*. Honolulu: University of Hawaii Press, 1985.

_____. *The Lapita Peoples: Ancestors of the Oceanic World*. Cambridge, Mass.: Blackwell Publishers, 1997.

Kyselka, Will. *An Ocean in Mind*. Honolulu: University of Hawaii Press, 1987.

Lang, John D. *Origin and Migrations of the Polynesian Nation*. 2nd ed. Sydney: George Robertson, 1877.

Lewis, David. *The Voyaging Stars: Secrets of the Pacific Island Navigators*. New York: W. W. Norton, 1978.

_____. *We, the Navigators*. Honolulu: University of Hawaii Press, 1972.

Rolett, Barry V. *Hanamiai: Prehistoric Colonization and Cultural Change in the Marquesas Islands, East Polynesia*. New Haven, Conn.: Dept. of Anthropology and Peabody Museum, Yale University, 1998.

Sharp, Andrew. *Ancient Voyagers in Polynesia*. Berkeley: University of California Press, 1963.

Sorrenson, M. P. K. *Maori Origins and Migrations*. Auckland: Auckland University Press, 1979.

Spriggs, Matthew. *The Island Melanesians*. Oxford: Blackwell Publishers, 1997.

Suggs, Robert. *The Island Civilizations of Polynesia*. New York: New American Library, 1960.

Terrell, John E. *Prehistory in the Pacific Islands*. Cambridge (Engl.): Cambridge University Press, 1986.

Thomas, Stephen D. *The Last Navigator*. New York: Henry Holt, 1987.

SONS OF SINBAD

Al Lawaty, Malallah bin Ali Habib (ed.). *Papers Submitted at the International Conference on the Silk Roads held at Sultan Qaboos University, Muscat, Sultanate of Oman, 20-21 November 1990.* Muscat: Ministry of National Heritage and Culture, 1992.

Aubet, Maria A. *The Phoenicians and the West: Politics, Colonies and Trade.* 2nd ed. Cambridge (Engl.): Cambridge University Press, 2001.

Bass, George F. (ed.). *A History of Seafaring; Based on Underwater Archaeology.* London: Thames & Hudson, 1972.

Bianquis, Th., C.E. Bosworth, E. J. van Donzel, and W. P. Heinrichs (eds.). *Encyclopedia of Islam.* New ed. Various volumes. Leiden: Brill Academic Publishers, 1986-.

Casson, Lionel. *The Ancient Mariners.* 2nd ed. Princeton, N.J.: Princeton University Press, 1991.

_____. *The Periplus Maris Erythraei: Text with Introduction, Translation and Commentary.* Princeton, N.J.: Princeton University Press, 1989.

_____. "Setting the Stage for Columbus." *Archaeology,* May-June 1990, pp. 50-55.

_____. *Ships and Seafaring in Ancient Times.* Austin: University of Texas Press, 1994.

Fantar, Mohamed. "The Phoenicians—Master Mariners of Antiquity." *The Unesco Courier,* Vol. 36, Dec. 1983, pp. 4-7.

Glubb, John B. 1988. Reprint. *A Short History of the Arab Peoples.* New York: Stein and Day, 1969.

Harley, John B., and David Woodward (eds.). *The History of Cartography,* Vol. 2, Book 1: *Cartography in the Traditional Islamic and South Asian Societies.* Chicago: University of Chicago Press, 1992.

Hawkins, Clifford W. *The Dhow—An Illustrated History of the Dhow and its World.* Lymington, Hampshire: Nautical Publishing Co., 1977.

Hourani, George F. *Arab Seafaring in the Indian Ocean in Ancient and Early Medieval Times.* Expanded ed. Princeton, N.J.: Princeton University Press, 1995.

Howarth, David. *Dhows.* London: Quartet Books, 1977.

Jenkins, Nancy. *The Boat beneath the Pyramid: King Cheops Royal Ship.* New York: Holt, Rinehart and Winston, 1980.

Landström, Björn. *Ships of the Pharaohs.* New York: Doubleday, 1970.

Lipke, Paul. *The Royal Ship of Cheops.* London: British Archaeological Report (International Series), 1984.

Ludmer-Gliebe, Susan. "Sinbads of the Sea." *Mercator's World,* Vol. 3, No. 6 (November/December 1998).

Markoe, Glenn. *Phoenicians.* Berkeley: University of California Press, 2000.

Martin, Esmond B., and Chryssee P. Martin. *Cargoes of The East: The Ports, Trade and Culture of the Arabian Seas and Western Indian Ocean.* London: Elm Tree Books, 1978.

Matthews, Samuel W. "The Phoenicians—Sea Lords of Antiquity." *National Geographic Magazine,* Vol. 146, No. 2 (August 1974), pp. 140-189.

Ministry of Information and Culture. *Oman, a Seafaring Nation.* Muscat: Ministry of Information and Culture, the Sultanate of Oman, 1979.

Morelon, Régis. "How Arab Sailors read the Stars." *The Unesco Courier,* Vol. 36, Dec.1983, pp. 8 -12.

Moscati, Sabatino (ed.) *The Phoenicians.* Milan: Bompiani, 1988.

Payne, Robert. 1992. Reprint. *The History of Islam.* New York: Barnes & Noble, 1959.

Severin, Timothy. *The Sindbad Voyage.* New York: Putnam, 1983.

Villiers, Alan. *Sons of Sinbad.* New York: Scribner, 1969.

_____. *Monsoon Seas; The Story of the Indian Ocean.* New York: McGraw-Hill, 1952.

Vinson, Steve. *Egyptian Boats and Ships.* Princes Risborough, Buckinghamshire: Shire Publications, 1994.

Young, George. *Constantinople.* New York: Barnes & Noble, 1992.

THE DRAGON AT SEA

Blunden, Caroline, and Mark Elvin. 1994. Reprint. *Cultural Atlas of China.* New York: Facts on File, 1983.

Donnelly, Ivon A. *Chinese Junks and Other Native Craft.* Shanghai: Kelly & Walsh, 1924.

Dreyer, Edward L. *Early Ming China: A Political History 1355-1435.* Stanford: Stanford University Press, 1982.

Grousset, René. 1992. Reprint. *The Rise and Splendour of the Chinese Empire.* Berkeley: University of California Press, 1953.

Levathes, Louise. *When China Ruled the Seas: The Treasure Fleet of the Dragon Throne 1405-1433.* New York: Simon & Schuster, 1994.

Ma Huan. *Yingyai Shenglan: The Overall Survey of the Ocean's Shores [1433].* Translated by J.V.G. Mills. Cambridge (Engl.): Hakluyt Society, 1970.

Maitland, Derek, and Nik Wheeler. *Setting Sails. A Tribute to the Chinese Junk.* Hong Kong: South China Morning Post, 1981.

Mathers, William, and Michael Flecker (eds). *Archaeological Report: Archaeological Recovery of the Java Sea Wreck*. Annapolis, Md.: Pacific Sea Resources, 1997.

Merson, John. *The Genius that was China—East and West in the Making of the Modern World*. Woodstock, N.Y.: The Overlook Press, 1990.

Nationaal Scheepvaartmuseum. *Scheve Schepen—De Vormenrijkdom van de Chinese Scheepsbouw*. Antwerpen: Nationaal Scheepvaartmuseum, 1993.

Needham, Joseph, Ling Wang, Gwei-Djen Lu, and Peng Yoke Ho. *Clerks and Craftsmen in China and the West—Lectures and Addresses on the History of Science and Technology*. Cambridge (Engl.): Cambridge University Press, 1970.

Needham, Joseph, and Ling Wang. *Science and Civilization in China*. Vol. III (1959), IV:2 (1965), IV:3 (1971), V (1986). Cambridge (Engl.): Cambridge University Press.

New China News. *The Grand Canal* (New China News). Hong Kong: South China Morning Post, 1984.

Oba, Osamu. "Scroll Paintings of Chinese Junks which Sailed to Nagasaki in the 18th Century and their Equipment." *The Mariner's Mirror* (reprint), Vol. 79 (1993), pp. 351-362.

Ronan, Colin A., and Joseph Needham. *The Shorter Science and Civilisation in China*. Volume 1. Cambridge (Engl.): Cambridge University Press, 1980.

_____. *The Shorter Science and Civilisation in China*. Volume 2. Cambridge (Engl.): Cambridge University Press, 1981.

Song, Yingxing. *Tian'gong Kaiwu, Chinese technology in the Seventeenth Century*. Translated by E-Tu Zen Sun and Shiou-Chuan Sun. University Park: The Pennsylvania State University Press, 1966.

Swanson, Bruce. *Eighth Voyage of the Dragon: A History of China's Quest for Seapower*. Annapolis: Naval Institute Press, 1982.

Temple, Robert, and Joseph Needham. *The Genius of China: 3,000 Years of Science, Discovery and Invention*. New York: Simon and Schuster, 1986.

Underwood, Horace H. 1979. Reprint. *Korean Boats and Ships*. Seoul: Yonsei University Press, 1934.

UNESCO Quangzhou International Seminar on China and the Maritime Silk Road Committee. *China and the Maritime Silk Route*. Quangzhou: Fujian People's Publishing House, 1994.

Wood, Michael. *Legacy: A Search for the Origins of Civilization*. London: Network Books, 1992.

Worcester, G. R. G. *Sail and Sweep in China*. London: Her Majesty's Stationery Office, 1966.

_____. *The Junks & Sampans of the Yangtze*. Annapolis: Naval Institute Press, 1971.

WOODEN SHIPS AND IRON MEN

Albuquerque, Luis de. *Instruments of Navigation*. Lisbon: National Commission for the Commemoration of the Portuguese Discoveries, 1988.

Albuquerque, Luis de, Max Justo Guedes, and Gerald Lombardi (eds). *Portugal-Brazil: The Age of Atlantic Discoveries*. Lisbon: Bertrand Editora, 1990.

Allen, Oliver E. *The Windjammers*. Alexandria, Va.: Time-Life Books, 1978.

Bailey, James. *The God-Kings & The Titans: The New World Ascendancy in Ancient Times*. New York: St. Martin's Press, 1973.

Bell, Christopher. *Portugal and the Quest for the Indies*. New York: Barnes & Noble, 1974.

Boorstin, Daniel J. *The Discoverers*. New York: Random House, 1985.

Boxer, Charles R. *The Portuguese Seaborne Empire, 1415-1825*. New York: Alfred A. Knopf, 1969.

Braudel, Fernand. *The Perspective of the World*. New York: Harper & Row, 1984.

Brouwer, Norman. *International Register of Historic Ships*. Annapolis: Naval Institute Press, 1985.

Casson, Lionel. *The Ancient Mariners*. 2nd ed. Princeton, N.J.: Princeton University Press, 1991.

_____. *Ships and Seafaring in Ancient Times*. London: British Museum Press, 1994.

Chapelet, Roger, Luís G. G. Marrecas Ferreira, A. Teixeira da Mota, and José Fernandes Martins e Silva. *Sagres, The School and the Ships*. Lisbon: Edições Culturais da Marinha, 1985.

Cohat, Yves. *The Vikings: Lords of the Seas*. New York: Harry N. Abrams, 1992.

Culican, William. *The First Merchant Venturers: The Ancient Levant in History and Commerce*. New York: McGraw-Hill, 1966.

Cuyvers, Luc. *Into the Rising Sun: Vasco da Gama and the Search for the Sea Route to the East*. New York: TV Books, 1999.

Domingues, Francisco C. *The India Run*. Lisbon: CTT Correios de Portugal, 1998.

Doumas, Christos, and Alexander Doumas. *Santorini: The Prehistoric City of Akroteri*. Athens: Editions Hannibal, 1988.

Fitzhugh, William, and Elisabeth I. Ward (eds.). *Vikings: The North Atlantic Saga*. Washington: Smithsonian Institution Press, 2000.

Furber, Holden. *Rival Empires of Trade in the Orient, 1600-1800*. Minneapolis: University of Minneapolis Press, 1976.

Gardner, Brian. *The East India Company*. New York: Dorset Press, 1971.

Greenhill, Basil. *The Life and Death of the Merchant Sailing Ship 1815-1965*. London: Her Majesty's Stationery Office, 1980.

Hale, John R. *Renaissance Exploration*. New York: W. W. Norton, 1968.

Haywood, John. *Dark Age Naval Power: A Re-assessment of Frankish and Anglo-Saxon Seafaring Activity*. London: Routledge, 1991.

Jones, Gwyn. *A History of the Vikings*. Rev. ed. Oxford: Oxford University Press, 1984.

Kemp, Peter. *The History of Ships*. London: Orbis Publishing, 1978.

Kemp, Peter, and Richard Ormond. *The Great Age of Sail*. New York: Facts on File Publications, 1986.

Koza, Thaddeus. *Tall Ships*. East Hartford: Tide-mark, 1996.

MacGregor, David R. *Merchant Sailing Ships: 1775-1815*. Annapolis: Naval Institute Press, 1988.

_____. *The Tea Clippers: Their History and Development, 1833-1875*. 2nd ed. Annapolis: Naval Institute Press, 1983.

Manchester, William. *A World Lit only by Fire: The Medieval Mind and the Renaissance*. Boston: Little, Brown, 1992.

Marshall, Michael. *Ocean Traders: From the Portuguese Discoverers to the Present Day*. New York: Facts on File Publications, 1990.

McGowan, Alan. *Tiller and Whipstaff: The Development of the Sailing Ship, 1400-1700*. London: Her Majesty's Stationery Office, 1981.

_____. *The Century before Steam: The Development of the Sailing Ship 1700-1820*. London: Her Majesty's Stationery Office, 1980.

McGrail, Sean. *Rafts, Boats and Ships from Prehistoric Times to the Medieval Era*. London: Her Majesty's Stationery Office, 1981.

Miller, Russell. *The East Indiamen*. Alexandria, Va.: Time-Life Books, 1980.

Ministry of Culture. *A Voyage into Time and Legend aboard the Kyrenia Ship*. Athens: Hellenic Institute for the Preservation of Nautical Tradition, 1987.

Morrison, John. *Long Ships and Round Ships: Warfare and Trade in the Mediterranean 3000 BC-500 AD*. London: Her Majesty's Stationery Office, 1980.

Natkiel, Richard, and Antony Preston. *Atlas of Maritime History*. New York: Facts on File Publications, 1986.

Olsen, Olaf, and Ole Crumlin-Pedersen. *Five Viking Ships from Roskilde Fjord*. Copenhagen: The National Museum, 1978.

Parry, John H. *The Discovery of the Sea*. New York: Dial Press, 1974.

Sandars, N. K. *The Sea Peoples: Warriors of the Ancient Mediterranean, 1250-1150 B.C.* Rev. ed. London: Thames & Hudson, 1985.

Spiers, George, and Peter Stanford (ed.). *The Wavertree*. New York: South Street Seaport, 1969.

Throckmorton, Peter (ed.). *The Sea Remembers; Shipwrecks and Archaeology from Homer's Greece to the Rediscovery of the Titanic*. New York: Weidenfeld & Nicolson, 1987.

Thubron, Colin. *The Ancient Mariners*. Alexandria, Va.: Time-Life Books, 1981.

Tooley, R. V. *Maps and Map-Makers*. 7th ed. New York: Dorset Press, 1987.

Van Gelder, Roelof, and Lodewijk Wagenaar. *Sporen van de Compagnie: De VOC in Nederland*. Amsterdam: De Bataafsche Leeuw, 1988.

Williams, J. E. D. *From Sails to Satellites: The Origin and Development of Navigational Science*. Oxford: Oxford University Press, 1992.

Wood, Peter. *The Spanish Main*. Alexandria, Va.: Time-Life Books, 1979.

INDEX

AMERICA

MAR

Circulus Arcticus

SEPTEN-

Afores Ins.
at Flandricæ.

DEL

TRIONALIS.

Nova Anglia.
Nova Belgium.

Arcadia

Tropicus Cancri.

Virginia

Florida

NORT.

HIS-
PANIA

Sinus
Mexicanus.

NOVA

MAR

DEL

Acamani

Carribana
GVIANA

Circulus Æquinoctialis

OCEANUS

AMERICA

ZUR.

PERVVI-
ENSIS.

MERI

DIO

Tropicus Capricorni.

MARE

PACIFICUM.

NA

TVR

LIS

Rio de la Platn

ZELANDIA
NOVA

Fretum Magellanicum

Circulus Antarcticus

Syftema Mundi ju.
mentem Claudii P
lemai Alexand.

AVSTRALIA Incognita

MARE
TARTARI

CVM.

TERRA